D0268255

Property Magic

6th revised and updated edition

How to buy property using
other people's time, money
and experience

Simon Zutshi

Property Magic

First published in 2008.
Sixth Edition published in February 2018 by

Panoma Press Ltd
St Vincent Drive, St Albans, Herts, AL1 5SJ, UK
info@panomapress.com
www.panomapress.com

Book Design and layout by Neil Coe.

Printed on acid-free paper from managed forests.

ISBN 978-1-784521-28-8

This book is available online and in bookstores.

Printed in the UK by TJ International Ltd, Padstow, Cornwall

FOREWORD

Every year I am fortunate enough to be asked to speak at property and wealth events all over the world. As can be expected, the knowledge and successes of the promoters and speakers varies tremendously from event to event. I met Simon Zutshi in October 2008 when I was the guest speaker at his 'Property Magic Live' weekend seminar in London. Not only was the organisation and production first class, but I was struck by Simon's knowledge of the subject, his willingness to share, and his passion for property in general. The event was truly magical. Simon made this possible by surrounding himself with a great team and great participants.

In essence, that is what 'Property Magic' is all about – creating a great team. Property investing can be a lonely pursuit if you are doing it on your own. However, it does not have to be that way. This book explains how to surround yourself with a power team and how to find people who can help you achieve your property investment goals. By leveraging other people's time, money and experience, you can build a solid property portfolio much more quickly and easily than doing so on your own.

Simon is an experienced, successful investor. More importantly for you, however, he is a great mentor and teacher. In this book he simplifies property investing concepts and clearly explains the steps you need to take. This book gives you all the information you need to buy property ethically, well below market value from motivated sellers. Having personally met many of the Property Mastermind delegates who, with Simon's guidance, have taken action and achieved incredible results, I know that if you study and adopt these principles, you too can achieve great success.

It does not matter what is happening to the economy in general, or the property market in particular; now is always a good time to invest in property. This book shows you how to educate yourself, conduct adequate research, buy for the long term, negotiate an advantageous price, generate positive cash flow from day one, and buy in an area with strong rental demand. All that is left to do is take action.

Successful investing,

Dolf de Roos
Phoenix, Arizona

www.dolfderoos.com

Author of the New York Times' and international best seller, *Real Estate Riches*

Contents

Understanding the property market

The changing property market

The property market had changed dramatically since I first sat down to write *Property Magic* in December 2007. All around the world, the market had been booming for many years. Here in the UK, property prices had gone up so much (faster than rents were going up) that it was becoming difficult to find properties that stacked up to give positive cash flow. The Bank of England Interest Base Rate was 5.75%, and we were just starting to see the effect of the Global Financial Crisis, noticeably with the demise of the UK mortgage lender Northern Rock the month before.

I don't think anyone would have been able to predict the changes that have happened since then. Yes, we were expecting the market to slow and show a small correction because it was overheated, but I doubt anyone predicted the dramatic effects this would have, particularly on the global mortgage market.

In the first edition of *Property Magic* I explained in detail a strategy that we were using at the time to buy property, 'No Money Down' (NMD). This method of acquisition required using literally none of your own money. It was achieved by purchasing a property from a motivated seller at a genuine 15%+ discount off the open market value, using short-term bridging to 100% finance the purchase, then remortgaging it the same day to the full value, to repay the bridging. The net result was that you would own a property with 15% equity and an 85% investment mortgage, which was the standard Loan to Value for an investment mortgage at that time. Sometimes you would get to walk away with cash in your pocket and with a tenant in the property from day one, creating yourself a positive cash flow straight away. You could literally get paid to buy a property. Those were the days.

It was a very simple and yet powerful strategy that enabled you to gain free equity in property like magic, "Property Magic". At the time, there were some cynical people who just didn't believe it was possible, despite the fact that many investors, myself and my students, were all doing it. That's one of the reasons I wrote this book in the first place, to provide a step-by-step guide explaining exactly what to do.

Rather frustratingly, two months after the publication of the first edition, the particular mortgage lender who was offering this product – which made the same-day remortgage possible – decided to withdraw the product from the market.

For some investors, who only had this one strategy, this was the end of NMD deals. Many investors, who were very successful before the Global Financial Crisis, failed to adapt their strategy to the changing market conditions and literally stopped buying property for many years. As a result, they missed one of the best property buying opportunities of that decade.

We, on the other hand, adapted, changed strategy and found other ways to buy property using other people's money. That is what professional investors do. We adapt to the changing environment and find innovative ways to make the most of the current market conditions. 2008 to 2010 was a great time to buy property as long as you knew what you were doing.

Since publishing the first edition of *Property Magic* in February 2008, the property market has crashed, then recovered, and changed so much that I decided it would be useful and important to frequently update this book, to ensure that you, the reader, have the latest, most relevant information as to how you can successfully invest in the UK property market. The edition you are now reading is the 6th revised and fully updated, 10th anniversary edition. Although the contents are mainly about investing in the UK for people who are either based here or investing here from overseas, the basic concepts of finding and helping motivated sellers work all over the world.

Before we get into the main content of the book, I think it will be useful to set the scene and explain what has happened to the UK property market and what could happen, so that you fully appreciate why "now" is such a good time for you to be investing in the residential property market, as long as you know what you're doing.

Property Cycles

The UK housing market is cyclical, just like every other market. It goes up and it goes down. The long-term trend in the UK is up, due to the reasons I will outline later in this chapter.

The fluctuation in house prices is due to short-term changes in supply and demand which are influenced by factors such as interest rates, availability of finance, government legislation, the media and the effect it has on public sentiment, level of employment, and the economy in general.

When investing in property, many people apply a policy of 'Buy Low and Sell High', a strategy borrowed from stock market investing. While there is nothing wrong with the concept behind this strategy, as you will certainly make money if you get it right, I have two fundamental issues with it.

1. It is very hard to establish when a market is truly at the top or bottom, so my view is: why guess, when it can be risky if you get it wrong?

2. I much prefer the idea of holding property long term to benefit from the significant capital growth rather than taking short-term profits by trading property. There are also tax benefits to holding rather than selling, which we will look at in Chapter 1.

What causes prices to crash?

The UK is a relatively small but popular island, with not enough housing to accommodate the increasing population, which is why the long-term trend in prices is upward. So why did the growth in property prices start to slow in 2007, and then crash in 2008? Essentially, this was due to a combination of a fall in demand and an increased supply of property at the same time, causing the fall in property prices.

There was a boom in house prices from 2001 to 2007, mainly fuelled by the ease of obtaining finance. In this period, many people who were previously unable to obtain mortgages were suddenly able to buy their own homes. Bad credit was not a problem and even those unable to prove an income were able to self certify, which meant simply declaring that they could afford their mortgage payments. As well as the increase in home ownership, there was a greater awareness of how to make money from property, sparked by the plethora of television programmes, which brought the idea of property investing to the general public. The increased availability of investment or Buy to Let (BTL) mortgages made it very easy to borrow money to buy investment properties, with lenders offering up to 90% Loan to Value (LTV) for BTL mortgages.

Towards the end of this boom period, as prices shot up, investors found that although rents were rising, they were not in line with the increases in property prices. It soon reached a point where investments just didn't stack up because the purchase prices were too high compared to the rent that was achievable. This inability to get property to stack up resulted in many professional property investors deciding to stop buying.

The other group of individuals who usually fuel the property market are first-time buyers, who also found that they couldn't afford to purchase at the higher prices, and so also stopped buying. The overheated prices resulted in a decline in demand for property towards the end of 2007 and into 2008.

On the supply side, there were several factors in 2007 that resulted in an increased supply of property for sale in the UK. First of all, in the summer of 2007, the UK government introduced Home Information Packs (HIPs) with the purpose of making the buying and selling process more reliable. Anyone selling a property after a certain date would need to pay for a HIP in order to market their property. What actually happened was that people who were thinking about putting their property on the market rushed to do so before the deadline and so avoided paying for a HIP. As you can imagine, the market was swamped with properties for sale. The requirement for HIPs was dropped by the government elected in 2010.

Also in late 2007, the effect of the Global Financial Crisis had hit the UK. Banks and mortgage lenders suddenly became very cautious about who they would lend money to. This mainly affected home owners with adverse credit, and investors with properties which had come to the end of fixed-rate and discounted mortgages, who then found themselves unable to re-mortgage to cheaper products. Suddenly these people were paying a lot more for their borrowing than before, and so many decided to sell their property to diminish the liability, rather than risk getting into difficulty which could ultimately result in the repossession of their property.

Basic economics tells us that when prices get too high, demand will fall off and prices will drop until they reach a level where people start to buy again.

With an average drop of 20% in prices, property was suddenly much more affordable. Even though property had come down in value to this more affordable level, most first-time buyers and many property investors still didn't buy due to the fear of further price falls, stimulated by the media.

That said, most lenders reported that, on average, UK house prices rose by approximately 8% in 2009. This, of course, was the average growth rate, mainly fuelled by rises in London, whereas in some parts of the country prices were still falling. A point to note here is that you need to be very careful when looking at *average* prices because that's exactly what they are:

a UK-wide average and not necessarily a correct reflection of the area where you may be buying your investment properties.

Will the market continue to rise?

No one really knows when a market will peak or bottom out. However, since 2009 the UK market has been steadily going up. In the last few years, the London property market in particular has boomed, and in most parts of the UK prices are now higher than they were at the end of 2007, which was the peak of the last boom.

So what is going to happen over the next few years? At the time of writing this sixth edition of *Property Magic*, there is a lot of uncertainty in the UK property market. The London market has slowed, despite continued investment from overseas. No one really knows what the impact will be on the UK economy when it finally withdraws from the European Union as a result of the Leave Vote in the BREXIT referendum.

The implementation of Section 24 tax changes in April 2017 means that higher-rate tax payers will now pay a lot more tax on any investment properties held in their own name. This has caused many people to question whether it is still a good idea to invest in property.

The other factor which could have a huge impact on the property market would be a rise in interest rates. The Bank of England base rate was cut to a record low of just 0.5% in March 2009. Many landlords who owned property at that time, including myself, have become very accustomed to strong positive cash flow from their property, purely thanks to these low interest rates. There was then a further reduction to 0.25% in August 2016. However, as the economy recovers and inflation goes up, at some point interest rates will go up. The first interest rate rise was in November 2017 when the Bank of England raised the base rate by 0.25% to 0.5%. This was expected to be the first of several small rises over the next few years. Higher interest rates, combined with more tax on investment properties, will means that the cash flow for some landlords will move from positive into negative. At this point many landlords, particularly those with single-let properties, may consider selling some or all of their portfolio. I predict that if interest rates continue to go up in the next two years, then at some point in 2019, or 2020 by the latest, we could see the property market flooded by investment properties for sale, and so the market may experience another dip in property prices.

Why invest in property now if there might be another crash in a few years time?

You have to accept that market booms are followed by market crashes, which are then followed by market booms, and so on. One of the questions I am often asked is: "If there might be another market crash, should I wait until then to buy?" This is a logical question but one based on the assumption that you buy at full-market value. Indeed, if you do pay full-market value for your investments, then yes, you could wait until the market crashes again and bottoms out – but good luck in predicting exactly when that might be!

However, the strategy of buying at full-market value is not the best way to invest, as you will discover later in this book. Where possible we look to purchase our investment properties from motivated sellers who might be flexible on the price or the terms of the sale. If you can purchase your investments with a big enough discount, it doesn't matter if prices fall further, as you will have an equity buffer.

When the market is falling, it is easier for you to negotiate bigger discounts off the property prices, because there are fewer buyers in the market and some vendors will be keen to dump their property before it falls much more in value. I really do believe that the next few years could be the buying opportunity of this decade, if you are ready and know what to do.

Once property prices bottom out and then start to rise again, it is always harder to obtain such large discounts. However, it is important to understand that there will always be motivated sellers no matter what is happening to the market.

The purpose of this book is to demonstrate what you could achieve in your property journey and to inspire you to take action. Now is always a great time to buy property as long as you know what you are doing. If you are going to be investing in property then I suggest you follow my five golden rules, which will help you maximise your return and minimise the risks.

Five Golden Rules of Investing

1. Always buy from motivated sellers

Instead of looking for a property you like and then negotiating with the seller, a smarter strategy is to look for motivated sellers who will be flexible on the price and/or the terms of the sale, and then decide if you want to buy that particular property. If they are prepared to sell at a discount for a quick sale, the amount of discount will vary depending on the motivation of the seller and the general market conditions. In a rising market you may be happy with a 15% to 20% discount. In a falling market you would want a bigger discount of 25% to 40% to give you more of a safety buffer in case prices come down further.

Just to be clear here, I am not saying that you always need to get a discount off the sales price. Sometimes property is already a great buy at the full asking price because it may already have been lowered for a quick sale. This is where knowing the values in your local market is really important so that you can spot a good deal when you see it. Many investors get fixated about buying below market value, which means they could miss out on potentially profitable deals because they don't think they should pay the full asking price. If it is a good deal, I will sometimes pay the full asking price and more, especially if I can add value to the property.

We also need to recognise that some sellers may not be able to offer you a discount because there is no equity in their property. However, if they are motivated, they may be more flexible on the terms of the sale, for example, when you actually pay them for the property. Price is not the only factor in negotiation. This means you may be able to use strategies such as 'Exchange with a Delayed Completion', or 'Purchase Lease Option' as described in Chapter 6. These strategies only really work if the seller is motivated.

The main theme in this book is how to find, understand and help these motivated sellers by reaching an ethical win/win solution for all involved.

2. Buy in an area with strong rental demand

You need to accept that as a landlord, you may occasionally have void periods in your property, which is when you have no tenants. During these void periods you have no income, which means you have to cover the costs of owning the property yourself. Your investment then becomes a liability, rather than an asset. However, you can dramatically reduce potential void periods by only buying property in an area with strong rental demand. You want to ensure that if your current tenants decide to leave the property, you can quickly and easily rent it to new tenants at the full-market rent. A general rule of thumb is to buy properties in areas with strong local employment and good transport links with local facilities and amenities.

When you know how to do it, you can easily assess the true rental demand in any area, by using the internet to find like comparisons, speaking to local letting agents, and even placing dummy adverts to test rental demand.

If you are not sure about the rental demand in an area, then I would suggest that you don't buy the property in order to avoid longer than expected void periods, which will cost you money. Due diligence is very important before you make any investment decisions.

3. Buy for positive cash flow

This is a very important rule. As a property investor you should aim to buy investment properties that not only pay for themselves, but also make a cash profit (positive cash flow) each month. There are running costs associated with owning a property, but the basic concept is that the rent you receive from your tenants more than covers all of the costs. In Chapter 5 I will explain more about renting out your property to maximise your rental income.

Unfortunately, when markets are booming, many investors will purchase properties which would only just "wash their face", where the rent would just about cover the monthly costs. Even worse than this, some speculators will buy properties that have negative cash flow, whereby the rent does not cover the monthly costs, in the hope that they will profit by prices continuing to rise. This means that the owners have to subsidise their properties each month, which is not a good position to be in, especially if you have a lot of properties like this.

If your investment properties make a positive cash flow each month, then it does not matter if property prices fall in the short term, because you can afford to hold them until the market recovers. One of the reasons many people lost money in the 2008 property market crash was because they owned properties which they had to put money into each month. If they could not afford to keep subsidising their property each month, then they had to sell at the worst time when prices had crashed and so they lost money.

You should only ever buy property where each month there is a profit from the rental income you receive after paying all of the expenses, including mortgage payments, insurance, repairs and management fees. Positive cash flow is king.

Although we expect property prices to rise in the long term, if you buy your investments 'as if prices will never go up again', you will be forced to buy only properties which give you great cash flow now. Extra cash flow will help you to build up a safety buffer, and help you cover potential rises in interest rates in the future.

4. Invest for the long-term buy and hold

Some investors like to buy and sell property to make a profit. This is called flipping property and can be very profitable in a rising market. However, each time you sell a property you will crystallise your profit, and you will never make any more money from that particular property. Whereas, if you buy and hold, you can make money from the rental profit each month as well as long-term capital growth. This way you work once and get paid forever by that property. More on this later in Chapter 1.

I have sold properties in the past and usually regretted it, having seen how much values go up in the long term. I believe the real profit in property is in buying and holding for the long term to benefit from significant capital growth. The key here is being able to afford to hold it, and this is why Rule No 3 (a positive cash flow) is so important, so that you don't have to subsidise ownership of the property.

If you plan to hold for the long term and your property is rented out creating a positive cash flow, you needn't be concerned by short-term fluctuations in price.

I am reluctant to sell property and will only do so for four reasons:

1. The equity tied up in the property is not generating a good return on investment so I could invest it elsewhere to make a better return.

2. If something has happened to the rental demand in the area since I first purchased the property, and I feel it may be difficult to rent it out in the long term.

3. If I wanted to raise funds to pay down some of my mortgages or build a war chest to make further purchases.

4. If I really needed the cash for whatever reason.

If you do sell a property, I suggest you reinvest some of the proceeds into another property that will give you a better return.

To conclude, I believe it is best to hold property for the long term. That is how you can become very wealthy and pass wealth on to future generations.

5. Have a cash buffer

When talking about Rule No 3, I mentioned investors who had to sell their properties because they could not afford to hold them. A problem I sometimes hear about is of properties occasionally getting damaged or just enduring wear and tear, making them difficult to rent. The landlord may not have the spare cash to make the necessary repairs and improvements and so the property remains void, which ends up costing the owner even more money. This becomes a vicious circle whereby the landlord can't afford to make the improvements because he has no rent coming in, and can't get any tenants because he can't afford to make the improvements. These landlords often become motivated sellers.

The way to avoid this potential problem is to make sure you always have a cash buffer set aside to cover unexpected expenses. In reality, you can get insurance to cover most of the potential issues, including a tenant not paying the rent. However, the more insurance policies you have, the higher your costs and so the less cash flow you will have each month.

I recommend you have a cash buffer in place, which you can use if need be. This could be cash in your bank, a clear credit card, or some cash in someone else's bank that you have agreed you can borrow if necessary. The size of this buffer depends on your personal level of risk. A few thousand pounds per property might be a good idea. This will help you avoid becoming a motivated seller yourself.

Long-term view of property prices

If you consider property investing as a long-term investment, then short-term price fluctuations should not be a concern, as long as you have carefully followed my Five Golden Rules of Investing, particularly rules No 2 and No 3.

Despite these occasional short-term fluctuations in the UK property market, the long-term trend is up, due to the fundamental reason that demand is greater than supply.

We live on a very popular island with limited space and an increasing population. A significant part of the countryside is Green Belt and so protected from development, and yet demand for accommodation continues to increase due to immigration, increased life expectancy, people living alone, rising divorce rates and changing social demographic trends, such as more young people going to university.

Although the demand for accommodation is ever mounting, the number of new homes being built each year slowed dramatically due to the downturn in the market in 2008. When the property market starts to rise again it always takes some time for the building industry to gear up to full building capacity.

If we are not building enough houses fast enough then what do you think will happen to property prices and the demand for rental accommodation?

Over the last 60 years, property prices in the UK have, on average, doubled every seven to nine years. Remember this is an average, and it does not happen EVERY seven to nine years. I believe we could see prices double again in the next 10 years but we shall have to wait and see.

Risks of investing

A word of caution before we continue. It would be unfair of me just to tell you about all the positives involved in property investing and not to mention the risks and downside.

Some people do lose money when investing in property. Property prices go down as well as up, as I have already explained. You might get void periods or tenants who don't pay you rent, or who even damage your property. These are some of the risks you need to be aware of. However, there are risks associated with anything you do in life. I believe if you educate yourself and do your research, you can mitigate many of the risks that you may encounter.

There is one particular risk that I have already mentioned but want to mention again and explain what you can do to minimise this particular risk.

This risk is the possibility of future interest rate rises. As a direct result of all the money that has been printed in the UK and around the world, we are likely to see high inflation at some point in the future. The Bank of England will probably use increased interest rates as a tool to control inflation.

It is worth noting here that inflation can be a good thing for us as property investors. Inflation means that the cost of living goes up, which also means the value of our properties rises as does the cost of renting a property, which means we receive more rental income. If we use interest-only mortgages to purchase our investment properties, although the amount we owe on each property remains the same for the duration of the mortgage term, the true value of this debt is eroded over time thanks to inflation.

I can't give you financial advice and this book is meant to be purely educational, but I will share my personal anti-inflationary strategy. On all the new mortgages I take out, and any re-mortgages, I am fixing my interest rate for as long as possible in an attempt to safeguard against potential high, unaffordable, interest rates over the next few years.

You should seek the advice of a qualified independent financial advisor and ask them to share their view on what could happen to interest rates over the next few years. Don't allow the fear of potential high interest rates to be another reason not to invest. There are ways of controlling property without even having a mortgage that I will share later in this book.

Before we continue

I would like to congratulate you for buying this book and more importantly for starting to read it. Would you believe that 50% of the books that are purchased are never even opened? I often meet people who say they purchased my book a year or so ago but never got round to reading it and then, when they did finally read it, they wished that they had done it years ago. So my recommendation here is simple. Read the book in full and then read it again.

I can't teach you everything in a book but I will expand your thinking and help you to recognise how property investing could change your life, which will in turn hopefully inspire you to take action. At the end of the day, it's down to you to take action to achieve the results you desire, but the good news is you don't have to do it on your own because that can be hard work.

The information that I share in this book is not just theoretical. Although the content is mainly about strategies which work here in the UK, the general principle of finding and helping motivated sellers is a concept that works anywhere in the world, although factors such as financing, taxation and regulations may of course be different in other countries. I have clients all around the world who have successfully implemented the concepts that I am going to share with you in this book.

Chapter 1:

You should be investing in property

You need to provide for your future

It's a sad fact that 98% of the population will die poor! As a nation we are all living longer, and that means we need more money to support us into our old age. In my opinion, it is unlikely that the state will be able to afford to support us. Most people can't rely on their company pension scheme. What this means for most people is that you will either have to keep working beyond the normal retirement age or accept a lower standard of living in your old age. That is, unless you do something about it now, which is probably why you are reading this book.

You have several options open to you:

1. You could start a business to generate some extra income.

2. You could invest in the stock market.

3. You could invest in property.

Personally I have done all three and I can confidently say that investing in property is by far the simplest and the safest and, for most people, can give them a much better return.

Property is one of the best investments you can make

People will always need somewhere to live. Here in the UK, we live on a popular island where the demand for accommodation is increasing. This means that, in the long-term, prices should continue to increase. Whilst this is a reassuring fact, it is not actually the biggest benefit of investing in property.

The main benefit of investing in property is the ability to invest using other people's money. The use of this gearing (or leverage) makes property investment stand head and shoulders above all other possible investments. Let's say you have a lump sum of £60k to invest. If you chose to put the money into the stock market, you could buy £60k worth of shares. If you selected your shares wisely and the company performed at the average growth rate of the stock market, which is a rate of 12% a year, then your investment of £60k would double to about £120k in just over five years' time. This would be a 100% return on your investment in five years. That's not bad – a rate of about 20% per year, thanks to the compounding. I think most people would invest more in the stock market at that kind of return, if only it was that easy to find good stocks. Of course, just like the property market, the stock market goes down as well as up.

If you took the same £60k and invested it in a property rather than shares, you would be able to purchase a £200k investment. This is possible through gearing and the use of other people's money. To buy an investment property, currently you need a 25% deposit, thus to purchase the £200k property you would need a deposit of £50k and the balance of £150k would come from the 75% LTV (Loan to Value), investment mortgage. Out of your £60k lump sum you would still have £10k left which would cover your purchase costs and maybe some furniture.

On average, over the last 60 years, property prices grow at about 9% per annum, but for this example, just to compare like with like, let's say that it grows at the same rate as the stock market and so use a growth rate of 12% per annum. (This was the average rate at which property prices grew from 2001 to 2007 but they were years of exceptional growth.)

If your investment property were to increase in value at 12% per year, just like the shares, it would also double in value in the same time period. The value of your property will have increased from £200k to £400k. However, you will have benefited from an increase in equity of £200k from your initial investment of just £60k, which means that you will have had a 333% Return On Investment (ROI). I am not aware of any other way to generate this kind of return safely on your investment.

In reality, with an average growth rate of 9% per year it might take eight years for your property to double in value. So 333% in eight years is still an average of 41.6% per year ROI. That is still a very strong return. Even at a very conservative growth rate of just 5% per annum, it would take 14 years for your property to double in value, giving you an average ROI of 23.8% per year. This is still more than you could make if your money was in a bank.

These rates of ROI are based on you putting in a 25% deposit. However, if you reduce the amount of deposit you put into the property, your ROI shoots up. In Chapter 3, I will share with you how to buy property and rapidly recycle the deposit, so that you have no money left in the deal, which means that you have an infinite ROI.

When using other people's money in the form of a mortgage, there is, of course, a cost to doing this. You will have to pay interest on the borrowed money. But here is the really clever part. You don't personally have to pay for the cost of borrowing, your tenant does! You don't live in the property and so you can let it out to someone else who pays you rent, which you use to cover all of the holding costs, such as mortgage interest, insurance, management fees, etc. This means that once you have an investment property, you can benefit from the long-term growth without having to make short-term contributions. It is like having someone else make contributions for you into your pension fund. This is as long as you make sure you buy a property in an area with strong rental demand, which stacks up, i.e. where the rental income more than covers all of the monthly expenses.

It is easy to understand why some people believe that you get a better return in the stock market than you do in property. The historical growth rate of the stock market has been an average of 12% per annum whereas the UK property market has only grown at a lower average rate of 9% per annum. Based on this one factor, many people assume that they get a better return in the stock market. They completely miss the point about gearing. Your property investment may well increase in value at a slower rate, but you get a better ROI as the growth is actually on a far larger investment, thanks to the fact that you can borrow money.

But is property really a safe investment? If you ask your bank for a loan, they will ask you why you want the money. If you tell them that you want the money to buy shares, they will tell you they can't help you. However, if you tell them you want to buy a property, they will invite you in to have a chat about it. This is because they know that property is a safe long-term investment, which is not the case with stocks and shares.

Now is a fantastic time to buy property as long as you know what you are doing. As you'll see later in this book, there are plenty of motivated sellers who may sell you their property for less than it is worth. If you buy at enough of a discount and recycle your deposit, then there is no limit to the amount of property you can buy.

With this in mind, why wouldn't you buy as much property as you can? Property can do so much for you. If you want, property can just generate some extra cash for you every month to help pay the bills or improve your lifestyle. If you buy enough of the right type of property, you can even generate enough passive income every month to replace your salary, which means that you will be financially independent and you won't need to work! If you no longer need to work, you can stop trading your time for money, and be free to do whatever you want with your time. Please be aware that it will take some effort and time to get to such a financially free situation, but it is perfectly possible. It took me eight years to achieve this because I was doing it on my own the hard way, making mistakes as I went along. However, with the correct specialist knowledge, mindset and supportive environment, some of my students have replaced their income in as little as six months! If you are fortunate enough to have a great job which you really enjoy and which pays you well, you may not want to give up work and that's fine, but property will help you build a solid pension for your future. Finally, you may want to invest for the future benefit of your family, to leave a legacy to your loved ones. Whatever your reasons, I think it is important to be clear in your own mind why you want to invest in property.

Take a moment now to consider the following:

- What would you like your property portfolio to do for you?

- How would you feel if, 12 months from now, you could choose how you spend your time thanks to the passive income from your property portfolio?

Why don't more people invest in property?

Most people recognise that investing in property is probably the best investment they can make, but unfortunately they don't do it. Something prevents them from taking the necessary action. What about you? Have you taken as much action as you should? Let's consider for a moment a few of the challenges that people face when thinking about investing in property.

Fear: We have all heard horror stories of people who have lost money when investing in property; of people who have had nightmare tenants. It is true, there can be problems associated with property investing but, in reality, most problems can be mitigated. It is only natural that people feel the fear and often it can paralyse them into a state of indecision. They are not sure what to do, so they do nothing.

Ignorance: Most people don't really understand what property can do for them and they are ignorant of why it is such a good investment. People don't bother to educate themselves because they don't know what they don't know. Or even worse, they think they know but actually they don't know. Some of the hardest people for me to educate are those who already have one or two investment properties and they think they know it all. You can never know it all because the property market is constantly changing and that's why I have updated this book so many times. I have been investing since 1995 and I don't claim to have all the answers.

Lack of knowledge: There are people who really want to invest in property but have no idea about how or where to start. When I first started investing in property, there were probably a handful of books about property investing, but that was it. I had to learn the hard way by trial and error. Today it is easy for you to learn from other successful investors through books, DVDs, seminars and even coaching and mentoring. There is no excuse for not knowing what to do. Aside from the problem mentioned, that often people don't know what they don't know, the second problem is that people are often not prepared to invest in their own education. Investing in yourself is probably the best investment you will ever make, closely followed by investing in property!

Lack of time: We are all busy and most people feel they don't have enough time to do everything they would like to do. Property investing is often one of those things that people know they should do, but feel they just don't have the time for. The irony is that if you invest just some of your time in building your property portfolio now, you will become financially independent in the future, which means that you can retire early and spend all of your time doing whatever you want to do, since you will not need to work for a living. We all have the same amount of time. It's a matter of how you decide to spend or invest your time.

Lack of money: This is one of the biggest barriers to property investing as most people are conditioned to believe that you need to have money to invest in property. If you have money, of course it is going to be easier to invest in property. However, if you know the correct strategy, you don't need much of your own money. After all, no matter how much money you have, at some point you will run out of your own funds and so you need to learn how to use other people's money to invest. These strategies will be explained in full later in this book.

Impatience: In today's society, many people have a very short-term view. If they don't get instant results they give up very easily. This can be a problem with property investing, which is a long-term investment and benefits come from a buy and hold strategy. You can make good cash flow from property right now, but the real value is in the long-term capital growth.

Tax: Incredibly, I've actually heard some people say that they don't want to invest in property because they will have to pay extra tax. Especially since we saw Section 24 introduced in April 2017, whereby higher-rate taxpayers now pay more tax if they own property in their own name. This has caused many amateur investors to wonder if it is still worth getting into property, and many long-term landlords are deciding to sell up and retire early. This actually presents an opportunity for us. Remember that you only have to pay tax when you make money, so surely having to pay lots of tax means you're quids in. Isn't that a good thing? The other important factor to consider here is that rich people usually don't pay very much tax. This is because rich people can afford to get good tax advice, which means that although they will pay some tax, generally they will pay fewer pence in the pound in tax than someone who is earning less money and cannot afford the right tax advice. Later in this book you will learn how to make tax-free money from your property, minimise your income tax and minimise the inheritance tax due on your estate. It you want to be wealthy, you not only need to learn how to make money but also how to keep it, by legally minimising the amount of tax you pay.

Just for a moment I would like you to consider which of these factors may have limited you in the past, prevented you from investing in property and stopped you from taking action to secure your financial future. How much has it cost you in missed opportunity to allow these concerns and fears to get in your way? I suppose the fact that you are reading this book means you have decided to do something about it. I congratulate you on this decision, and look forward to accompanying you on your journey of discovery about property investment.

The opportunity for you to make a serious amount of money from the UK property market, and change your life forever, is very real and available to you right now. It all starts with raising your awareness of the possibilities, and inspiring you to take action on the ideas and information I am sharing with you. I encourage you to read this book from cover to cover, and then read it again to get the most out of it. Your journey starts with education.

So what is your strategy?

When I first started to invest in property, I didn't have a strategy. I just thought that property was a good investment and so I started to buy, and I seem to have muddled through somehow. I think many people start like this, but if I was starting to invest now, I would certainly be very clear and focused on my strategy. You need to work out what you want property to do for you. Some property will give you strong capital growth, some investments will give you great cash flow, and occasionally, if you are lucky, you might get both. You need to think about what is important to you. What you ultimately want to achieve will shape your strategy, which will influence the type of property you purchase.

A vital part of your strategy planning is to consider your exit strategy. This will have a big effect on the structure within which you buy property, the type of property you buy, and maybe even the way you finance it.

Have you considered your exit strategy?

I have always understood that historically, on average, property prices in the UK double every seven to nine years. Based on this understanding, my initial exit strategy was very simple.

The idea was to start buying investment property where the rent would more than cover the costs and so give me a positive cash flow. I was quite successful at this, so that by the age of 32 I was financially independent, due to the income from my rental properties. I thought I would stop buying at some point and then just wait for my portfolio to double in value. Once the portfolio had doubled in value I was planning to sell half of the properties and use the proceeds from the sale to pay off all of the mortgages on the remaining half of my portfolio. I would then own the remaining properties outright and so would make a great positive cash flow, since I would have no mortgages to pay but would still receive the rental income from them. This seemed like common sense to me and I know that many investors have an exit strategy similar to this.

Consider a numerical example of this: Assume that you were able to buy 10 properties over a few years. If the average value of each property was £200,000, then the total value of your portfolio would be £2m. There would probably be mortgages on your portfolio of at least 75% LTV, which would equate to £1.5m of debt. In case you feel scared about having that much debt, remember that the cost of the debt should be more than covered by the rental income from your tenants.

Conservatively, it could take at least 10 years for the property market to double in value again. In that time, your 10 properties could each have doubled in value from £200,000 to £400,000. This means your total portfolio of 10 properties could be worth £4m. At this point, if you were to sell half of your portfolio you would raise £2m from the sale before tax and sales costs. By utilising your various capital gains allowances, you could end up with net revenue sufficient to completely clear the original £1.5m of debt and have some money left over. This would leave you with five properties valued at £400,000 each with no debt. Would you be happy with a £2m debt-free property portfolio?

This seemed like a great idea to me. However, after seeking expert tax advice, I realised that this was not a very tax-efficient strategy for two main reasons:

1. You would have to pay Capital Gains Tax on all the properties that were sold. There are ways of minimising your Capital Gains Tax but, in reality, if you were selling half of your portfolio, even if you stagger it over a number of years, there will be some tax to pay.

2. The second tax problem is Inheritance Tax. If you clear all your debts and own your properties outright, you will yield a large Inheritance Tax liability on your estate in the future.

This is in essence a good exit strategy, and I completely understand people wanting to pay down the mortgage debt, but it is not very tax efficient as you will have to pay lots of Capital Gains Tax and Inheritance Tax. I understand the importance of paying tax and contributing to society, but why pay more tax than you have to if there is an alternative, more tax-efficient strategy?

After seeking professional tax advice, I decided to change my strategy as follows: instead of selling half of my portfolio and using the sales proceeds to clear the mortgage debt, I have instead kept all of the property and its associated debt forever! I re-mortgage my property as it increases in value and as rental income will allow. The cash generated from a re-mortgage is tax-free because it is debt. This is how you can release money from your portfolio without selling it. There are two distinct tax advantages with this new exit strategy:

1. If you don't sell, you never pay Capital Gains Tax. At death, any Capital Gains Tax liability on your property portfolio is wiped out.

2. By constantly re-mortgaging your property and removing equity, you will be increasing your level of debt, which at the same time will reduce your net assets and so reduce potential Inheritance Tax liability on your estate.

Back to the numerical example:

Your 10 properties have each doubled in value from £200,000 to £400,000 in 10 years so that the total value of your portfolio is now £4m. The initial borrowing was £1.5m (75% LTV). If you increase the borrowing over the 10-year period by re-mortgaging each property at an appropriate time, then you would be able to withdraw a substantial amount of cash, tax-free, from your portfolio.

As you re-mortgage your portfolio over time, if you were to maintain the level of borrowing at 75% LTV, you would be able to borrow up to £3m against the portfolio value of £4m. With your original mortgages of £1.5m, this would be an increase in borrowing of £1.5m that you had taken out of your portfolio over a 10-year period. This works out to be an average of £150,000 tax-free money in your pocket each year. Would that help your lifestyle?

I would like to invite you to re-read this section now to make sure you understand it, as this information alone could save you hundreds of thousands of pounds in tax in the future. Then make sure you get some proper tax advice to understand your personal tax position.

There are two drawbacks to this strategy:

1. If you ever had to sell a property from which you have withdrawn substantial amounts of cash as the value had increased over time, it is possible that the Capital Gains Tax payable on the property may well be more than the profits generated from the sale of that property. It is important to make sure that you can hold onto these properties for life.

2. Prior to April 2017, you could offset all of your mortgage interest cost (on borrowing up to the value of the property at the time at which you first rented it out) against your rental income to reduce your paper profit and to pay less tax. However, now due to Section 24 you can not do this anymore and so you will pay more tax on your property rental income if you are a higher-rate taxpayer.

I had adapted my exit strategy to this considerably more tax-efficient model. This illustration is meant for educational purposes only. I have now had to adapt my strategy once again due to the April 2017 tax changes. As professional investors it is important you keep up-to-date with changes in the market conditions and adapt your strategy as necessary.

I recommend you should consult a qualified tax professional to give you advice based on your personal circumstances. A word of caution here: many tax experts don't understand property investing. So, as is always the case, you need to make sure the expert from whom you are seeking advice really understands property investing and ideally will also be an investor themselves, so that they understand exactly what you are aiming to achieve. Over the years, I have met numerous qualified and regulated Independent Financial Advisors (IFAs) who know absolutely nothing about property investing and so advise their clients not to invest in property. This is a real shame as their clients have missed out on significant capital value appreciation due to the lack of knowledge of the so-called professional advisor.

Buy as an individual or in a company?

I am often asked this question. As already mentioned, I am not qualified to give you tax advice and it does depend on your personal circumstances and your investing strategy. Prior to April 2017 we would say that if you wanted to buy and hold property for the long term and use the equity release strategy described, then buying as an individual would make more sense from a tax point of view. If you wanted to trade property, i.e. where you purchase it, renovate it and sell on for a profit, then a company structure may be more tax efficient.

However, if I was starting from scratch now, I would probably set up a property company to buy and hold my property portfolio. Buying in a company can be more expensive in terms of mortgage interest rates and arrangement costs, but I am sure that will change as the market becomes more competitive and more and more people buy through their property companies. With your own company, there are also many expenses that you can offset including the cost of property education and training.

If you are an expat. living overseas, or a foreign investor, wanting to invest in the UK, then the best way is definitely to set up a UK business with a UK bank account. (More on this later for overseas investors.)

I strongly recommend that you seek professional advice to structure your property investing in the most appropriate way for you.

You can do it – all you need is the right system

The good news is that anybody can invest in property. Property investment is like magic, in that it is quite simple when you know how to do it, and the results that you can achieve are incredible – also like magic! The purpose of this book is to show you not only what you can do, but how you can do it. Even better than that, you don't have to do it all on your own. The Mastermind Principle that I will share with you later in this book will show you how you can build your property portfolio using other people's time, money, knowledge and expertise.

The main focus of this book is on how you can buy property from motivated sellers. If you can purchase your investment properties below market value, you lock in profit on the day you buy, rather than having to wait for the long-term capital appreciation. You also give yourself a buffer against falls in the property value. Alternatively, you can purchase property at full value which requires some work doing to it, and hence add value, which is another way of locking in value when you purchase it.

The information is all here for you. All you need to do is put it into action. Unfortunately, this is where most people fail. They know what they need to do and they know they should do it, but they fail to take the necessary action. I believe this is because they don't have the right mindset. You can have all the strategies in the world, but if you don't have the correct attitude and mindset they will not work effectively for you. So, in addition to showing you what to do, I am going to use a part of this book helping you to work on your mindset and belief in what is possible, by sharing some inspirational case studies of what other people just like you have achieved.

Chapter 2:

You can buy property using none of your own money

There is a common belief that you need to have a lot of money to be able to invest in property. Whilst it is true that having money will make it much easier to invest, it is possible to invest without using any of your own money.

I meet investors all the time who have stopped buying because they have run out of deposits. They all seem to have a similar story. When they first realised how powerful property investing could be for them and for their financial future, they used all the money they could, from savings, inheritance or released equity from their home, to buy as many Buy-to-Let (BTL) investment properties as possible.

They used the maximum LTV borrowing so that they could make the most of their deposit money and spread it across as many properties as possible. The problem that all investors run into is that, no matter how much money they have for deposits, at some point they will run out, which is when most people stop buying because they don't know how to use other people's money.

When they run out of deposit funds most investors just sit back and wait. They wait until property prices have sufficiently risen for them to re-mortgage their investments to pull out some cash, which can then be recycled as deposits to buy even more properties, and so the cycle continues. This is a great strategy to build your portfolio over the long term, and certainly what I did when I was first building my property portfolio.

The main problem is that this is a long-term strategy and you have to wait for sufficient capital appreciation of the properties to be able to pull out money to fund your next purchase.

There is a two-part solution to this particular problem. Firstly, rather than using your own money for deposits, use other people's money instead. Secondly, you can recycle your deposit faster if you can reduce the amount of time required until there's sufficient equity in the property to refinance. This can be achieved by buying the property significantly below the true market value and/or adding value to the property such that, in a short period of time, the property can be refinanced to take out the initial deposit which could then be reused on further investments. We call this momentum investing.

In this chapter, we are going to explore this solution to show you how you can buy as many properties as you like using other people's money. But first let's make sure you understand some of the basic terminology related to financing your property investments.

Residential mortgages

When you buy your own home you take out a residential mortgage which generally requires a deposit of typically 10% to 25%. Your personal credit score and income are very important, particularly with the Mortgage Market Review (MMR) which came in from April 2014, to ensure people can afford their residential mortgages.

Prior to the Global Financial Crisis at the end of 2007, in some circumstances you wouldn't need any deposit at all because some banks would lend you up to 100% of the value of the property, if you had a good enough income. There were some lenders who would even lend as much as 125% of the value of the property. If you were buying your home for £200,000, they would actually lend you £250,000 so you could use the extra £50,000 to do whatever you wanted.

Some smart people took that extra 25% and used it for a deposit to buy a Buy-to-Let property, which they could rent out. Many not so wise people enjoyed that money, went on holiday, purchased cars, etc, only to find themselves in a predicament a few years later when they wanted to sell their home and move on. They then found the debt was far higher than the value of the property. This is one of the factors that helped cause the Global Financial Crisis in the first place. There are people who are still in negative equity now because of this irresponsible lending and borrowing.

Buy-to-Let mortgages

When you buy a property that is not your own home, you need a specialist BTL (Buy to Let) mortgage where the lender is aware that you will not be living there, but instead letting it out to tenants who will pay you rent.

The amount of mortgage you can obtain will vary depending on the mortgage market conditions. Most of the BTL properties I have purchased with 85% LTV mortgages, and even up to 90% LTV mortgages in some circumstances when the market was booming.

With the Global Financial Crisis, the mortgage market changed radically and the availability of investment mortgages reduced drastically, as did the LTV that lenders were prepared to lend against BTL investments. With maximum lending of 75% LTV, investors would need a 25% deposit. The maximum LTV available for BTL mortgages will naturally increase as the market recovers and the banks regain confidence.

Mortgages for people living outside the UK

If you currently live outside the UK but want to invest in property here, there are a few mortgage lenders who you can acquire BTL mortgages from. They will lend up to 75% LTV, however they will also need to see proof of your personal income and it's better if you are employed rather than self-employed.

Mortgages for foreign nationals living in the UK

If you are not originally from the UK but living here, then there are a few mortgage lenders from whom you can acquire BTL mortgages once you have a full two years of UK address history. They will lend up to 75% LTV but the amount of lending will be based very much on your personal income. They may use a multiple of your income (such as 4 x income) instead of the rental income calculation used for most BTL mortgages.

Please be aware that the mortgage market is constantly changing, so it's a great idea to use an independent mortgage advisor who has access to the full market so you can get best advice at the time you make your property purchase.

The difference between mortgages and re-mortgages

Although it may sound obvious, this is a key concept that many investors find very difficult to comprehend when they first learn about these creative strategies. As you discover later in this chapter, this is particularly relevant when using the Momentum Investing Strategy.

Normally, when you first buy a property you get a mortgage. If you own a property that you refinance it's called a re- mortgage. There is a fundamental difference between a mortgage and a re-mortgage. When you buy a property, the mortgage is generally based on the purchase price of the property or the value, whichever is lower. However, a re-mortgage is based on the value of the property and the purchase price is not so important.

Let me elaborate. Let's say you own a property that you want to refinance. You arrange for a re-mortgage of the property. The mortgage lender you choose would instruct a surveyor to conduct a valuation of the building. The surveyor will assess how much the property is worth but will very rarely ask you about the purchase price, because as it's a re-mortgage it doesn't really matter. It is all based on the value of the property. If the property is worth £240,000, the lender would probably give you a loan of 75% of the value, which in this case would be a loan of £180,000. A point to note here is that most BTL mortgage lenders in the UK will want you to own the property for six months before you are able to re-mortgage it. This is called "The Six Month Rule". Although, as the mortgage market improves, there are a few exceptions to this.

Now let's assume that you don't own this particular property but you are buying it at full market value. You would be buying the property for £240,000. The surveyor would come round to value the property and as it is a mortgage on this occasion, they would be interested in how much you purchased the property for and they would base the loan on that purchase price. A 75% LTV mortgage would mean that you could get a loan of £180,000, which is 75% of the purchase price. As usual with most purchases, you will be required to put in a 25% deposit, which in this case would be £60,000; nothing unusual about this so far.

Taking this example one stage further, let's say that although the house is worth £240,000, the motivated seller, who needs to sell their house quickly, has agreed to sell it to you for just £176,000. The surveyor would be sent to the property to conduct a valuation on behalf of your mortgage lender. Once the surveyor discovers how much you are paying for it, the lender would give you a mortgage based on that purchase price of £176,000. A typical 75% mortgage would give you a loan of £132,000 even though the property is worth £240,000. Remember, you would only get a mortgage of £132,000 because the mortgage is based on the purchase price not the value. This is unfortunate, because if you already owned the property and were to re-mortgage it, you would be able to get a loan of £180,000 as this would be 75% of the value.

A point to note is that some mortgage lenders may decline to lend to you if they believe this to be a distressed sale on the basis that you are buying the property for £172k even though it is worth £240k. This is because they don't want to be associated with helping "unethical investors" who take advantage of people in financial difficulty. This is rather hypocritical of the mortgage lenders, as they seem to be prepared to repossess these same people if they can't afford to pay their mortgage.

As you will see in Chapter 4, we believe in ethically investing so we help people solve their property problems and we benefit at the same time. Helping someone sell at a discount may actually be much better for them than being repossessed by the bank, which has all sorts of implications.

Momentum Investing

This is really important to understand because it is one of the key strategies that you can use to rapidly build your cash generating property portfolio. This strategy solves the problem of having to wait for the value of your property to increase before you can re-mortgage it. Once you understand and apply this technique, you will take years off the time required to acquire your portfolio.

Here is how it works: you purchase the property at the agreed £176,000 by using a £132,000 mortgage and a £44,000 deposit. Once you have owned the property for six months, you can refinance it. Based on the value of £240,000, you could apply for a re-mortgage of £180,000. This means you would get back your £44,000 deposit plus an extra £4,000, which will cover some of your refinance costs.

The only challenge is that you still tie-up the deposit for six months until you can re-mortgage the property and you also have increased costs due to having two surveys, two sets of legal costs and potentially two arrangement fees on the finance.

Another potential issue when you come to re-mortgage is that you may struggle to prove the true value at £240k if you originally purchased it just six months previously for £176k. To overcome this, it can be useful to obtain an independent RICS (Royal Institution of Chartered Surveyors) valuation before you purchase it to show the true value of £240k. Also, take some pictures before and after any work you do to clearly demonstrate that you have added value to the property. This may be as simple as a coat of paint and new carpets, which can dramatically transform the appearance of a property.

Here is a great example of Momentum Investing in practice.

CASE STUDY:
Curtis Jackson

I am a 27-year-old electrician from Nottingham. I first began investing in property just over a year ago, after seeing my best friend, Alex Seery, achieve staggering results using none of his own money whilst he was on the Property Mastermind Programme. I was very unfulfilled working in a job 6-7 days per week to make ends meet. This meant that I never had the time that I wanted to spend with my family and loved ones. I saw the power of property investing as a clear route for me to get to where I wanted to be. This made me commit to the decision of investing my life savings in my own education and I joined the 12-month Property Mastermind.

As I had no investing track record, I began to earn my stripes as a professional property investor by first gaining experience through doing a rent to rent deal. This worked really well and gave me the confidence to see if my father wanted to do a joint venture with me. I knew he had equity in his house (in which I grew up) and with the type of deals I was looking at there was potential to recycle all of the money using momentum investing. We sat down and discussed this before agreeing to do a joint venture together.

I live in Nottingham where the local council has introduced Article 4 direction, meaning that I wouldn't be able to buy a residential property and convert it into a House of Multiple Occupation (HMO). With this being the case, I chose to invest in the neighbouring city of Derby. I started to search for properties that I could buy BMV and add value to. This would then give me the uplift in value that I'd need in order to recycle all of the money back out of it.

I soon found one property on the internet that I believed had heaps of potential. It was a 3-bedroom terraced house which was only a 5-minute drive from Derby city centre.

The house was in need of refurbishment and this was reflected in the price of just £90k. This price jumped out at me immediately as a good deal, as I had already developed a good understanding of average house prices in this area. Even in its poor condition, I believed it to be worth well over £100k.

I was very excited and couldn't call the estate agent quickly enough to book a viewing. With some words of persuasion, I managed to book a slot for that same afternoon. With the agent stressing that they were squeezing me in, it was to my surprise that two other people turned up to also view.

Whilst there was a slight awkwardness at having others there at the viewing, I measured the loft and basement spaces which I then knew could be converted into living space. I also built as much rapport as possible with George the estate agent before asking him for the reason why the vendor was selling. He was very open in telling me that the couple who owned the house were getting a divorce and therefore were very motivated to put an end to their pain by selling the property as soon as possible. This all made sense as to why it was such a BMV deal. As soon as I arrived home from the viewing, I called the estate agent and offered the full asking price of £90k on condition that the property be removed from the market straightaway. George called me back to congratulate me on what was to be my first sale agreed property.

With the property purchase pending, the mortgage lender sent out a surveyor to check that the property was fit to lend on. The surveyor's report came back, with the lender then stating they would hold a £7.5k retention on the money they'd lend me until I had works completed. The list consisted of damp, roof works and a few other things which I saw as minor, seeing as I was already aware of them and had already allowed for them in the stacked refurb cost. Knowing full well that the vendors were motivated, I called George explaining that I didn't have the extra cash which was required in order to complete as the bank wouldn't lend it to me. Reminding him several times that serious works needed to be carried out at the property, I said that I simply needed the £7.5k deducted from the price in order to complete which was touching distance away as I'd already got everything else finalised. After he'd spoken to both of the vendors, I received a phone call from him the same day to confirm that my new offer had been accepted and that I was to purchase the property for £82.5k.

I met the local HMO officer at the property whilst the purchase was going through. He informed me that he believed the property was too small to be a 5-bed HMO as I'd hoped, however he told me that if all of the regulations and minimum room sizes were met, then I'd of course be granted the licence. This was good enough for me as I had done my measurements and knew that, with a basement conversion and part-loft conversion, we would transform the house into a 5-bed HMO whilst adding a huge amount of value by adding much more living space.

This was a perfect deal to do with my father as a joint venture. At 75% LTV minus the £7.5k retention, the mortgage lender loaned us £54,375. We had to put in the 25% deposit plus the extra £7.5k making this a total of £28,125. The refurbishment costs along with the cost of bills and expenses were £55k. Including stamp duty and all professional fees, the total amount my JV partner put in was £91k. The property became a fully-licensed 5-bed HMO with generous communal space and 3 shower rooms. At the point at which we'd owned the property for 6 months, we refinanced it. I met the surveyor on site and ambitiously named the valuation of £235k to him, emphasising the fact that we'd added around 35% to the property's internal living space. The valuation came back at £200k. At 80% LTV we were offered a remortgage of £160k. This meant we were able to clear the original mortgage and pay back £91k to my father. Not only did we get all of our money out, but we also had an extra cash profit of just over £15k which we split between us.

We split all of the cash flow and equity growth 50/50, which I do believe is the most decent and clean way of doing this type of JV deal, providing that each party brings value to the table.

A summary of the deal is as follows:

- Property sourced on www.rightmove.co.uk
- 3-bed house converted in to a 5-bed HMO
- Purchase price: £82.5k
- Refurb and expenses: £55k
- Total initial money required: £91k
- Valued at £200k after refurb and re-mortgaged to £160k so all money back plus £15,531 cash out
- Total rental income is £2,445 per month
- Monthly profit after costs is £1,480
- Monthly cash flow split 50/50 = £740pcm / £8,880pa

I am delighted to say that by firstly investing in myself, which in turn allowed me to invest in property, I have now secured four R2R deals and six JV purchases. These assets provide me with a passive income of £98k pa, being transmitted through my business which is systemised to allow me pretty much all of my time to myself. Joining the Property Mastermind has proved to be the single best decision of my life in terms of my improved financial status, personal growth and happiness, which I have achieved in such a short space of time.

What about commercial finance?

Depending on the type of property you are buying, you may well be able to apply for commercial finance. Typically this would be for properties such as Houses of Multiple Occupation (see more about these in Chapter 5) and is only relevant if you are an experienced landlord.

There are some key differences between traditional BTL mortgages and commercial finance. The first main point is that with commercial finance you can borrow 65% to 70% LTV as opposed to 75% with a BTL mortgage. However, and this is the really interesting point – the value of the property is not necessarily based on the bricks and mortar value but rather on a multiple of the rental income. What this means is that, if the property generates a very high rental income, then it may be possible to borrow more money than with a traditional BTL mortgage.

The second difference between BTL mortgages and commercial finance is that commercial lenders generally don't require you to own the property for six months before you re-mortgage it. This means you could buy a property then re-mortgage it with commercial finance just two or three months after purchase.

This is particularly relevant to Momentum Investing because it means that you can recycle your money even quicker.

Creative ways to buy property

As a sophisticated investor you need to keep up-to-date with the market and how it is changing. There will always be creative ways to buy property but they will change over time. Since writing the first edition of this book at the end of 2007 the market conditions have changed dramatically and the strategies we use to buy property have also changed.

Although you can't use it at the time of writing, as a point of reference and demonstration of creativity, it may be worth describing the 'No Money Left In' (NMLI) method of buying property that I detailed in the first edition of *Property Magic*.

You buy the property at the discounted rate for cash – not with your own money but using short-term bridging finance. Once you are the owner, you can re-mortgage the property on the same day with a re-mortgage based on the true value. As in the previous example, you would buy the property worth £240,000 for £176,000 and arrange a re-mortgage for £180,000, thus covering the entire purchase price and giving you £4,000 to cover your purchase costs. Purchasing the property in this manner means that you have acquired a property with £60,000 of equity, using none of your own money.

The methods of buying property with none of your own money are described later in this chapter, but before we consider these let's just look at a case study of the very first NMLI deal that I did back in 2006. The discount I achieved, through helping the seller to solve his problem, effectively gave me the equity for the deposit.

CASE STUDY:
My first NMLI purchase

My first NMLI property purchase was in Nottingham. The owner of this property (let's call him Bob) had been made redundant and he had slipped behind with the mortgage payments on his home. Bob also had an unsecured loan with the bank. He was paying a high rate of interest and could not keep up with repayments, and so slipped behind to the point that, when I first met him, Bob was about a month away from having his property repossessed.

I initially spoke to Bob on the telephone and agreed to go and have a look at the property and see if I could help him. I asked Bob what he wanted in return for his property. He made it clear that all he really wanted was to pay off all the debts and to have £2,000 left in his hand, and he wanted to rent back the property long term at an affordable rent.

His mortgage was £56,000 and his bank loan was £6,000. This meant that I was able to purchase the property for £64,000, which included the £2,000 Bob wanted in his hand. We both knew that this price was significantly below the true market value which was about £90,000.

To be honest, I couldn't quite understand why Bob was prepared to sell his property at such a discounted price. However, Bob had considered all the other options and selling the house was really the only thing he could do. He also wanted to be able to stay in the house as he had lived there for nearly 20 years. I asked Bob what he could afford to pay in terms of rent. He explained that he was not able to cover the cost of his mortgage and loan repayment at £800 a month, which is why he was facing repossession, but he could afford about £400 a month, if I was prepared to accept that as rent. The average market rent for this type of property in the area was more like £475 per month, but as he was selling the property to me at a big discount, I agreed to rent the property back to him at the discounted rent for as long as he wanted.

Having agreed the deal, I left Bob's house and immediately phoned my mortgage broker to instruct him to apply for the re-mortgage and arrange the survey on the property. Next I called my solicitor and instructed her to carry out the searches on the property. Finally, I also called a second solicitor and asked them to contact Bob to represent him in the sale of the property.

Based on my research, I estimated the property was worth between £90,000 and £100,000. I asked my mortgage broker to put a value of £95,000 on the re-mortgage application form. The lender's surveyor visited the property to carry out his valuation and agreed that the value was £95,000. Based on the value of £95,000, the lender was prepared to give me an 85% re-mortgage equivalent to £80,750. As you can see, the re-mortgage loan was much greater than the purchase price. This meant that I would be getting some tax-free cash out of the deal.

On the completion day, my solicitor used £68,500 in bridging to purchase the property. This covered the £64,000 required for the actual purchase and £4,500 to cover all of the purchase costs, which included the solicitors' fees on both sides, the cost of the bridging, and the finder's fee for the property. Once the property was in my name, the solicitor was able to use the funds from the re-mortgage to pay back the bridging and the balance of approximately £12,000 was sent to me. This meant that on my very first motivated seller purchase, I was able to pull £12,000 tax-free cash out of the deal and end up with a property worth £95,000 with £14,250 equity in it, and a tenant in the property from day one who, although paying slightly less than the market rent, was paying enough to cover all the monthly costs.

At the time, I was able to get an 85% LTV re-mortgage, but even with one at 75% LTV I would still have walked out with £2,750 in tax-free cash and had a mortgage of £71,250 and equity of £23,750. Still a great deal!

It is important to note here that the Financial Services Authority (which has now changed to the Financial Conduct Authority) and the UK government introduced some new legislation on 1st July 2009 regarding Sale and Rent Back (SARB), which although it was well intended, to protect the consumer, effectively means you can't do SARB anymore. If Bob called me now with the same problem, I might still be able to buy his property, but I would not be allowed to rent it back to him, which is what he really wanted. I am convinced this over-regulation means that properties have been repossessed from people who could have been helped by investors like you and me. The good news is that this restriction only currently applies to the UK. Many of my students outside the UK are still able to help sellers with this Sale and Rent Back strategy where appropriate.

Is it easy to find this kind of deal?

That was a pretty good first motivated seller purchase. You may like to know how I found that deal in the first place? Well, I didn't find it myself. I purchased the lead from another investor who had found Bob but didn't want to go ahead with the purchase because the property was out of his area and not the kind of property he would normally buy. I paid a fee of 2% (of the purchase price) plus VAT for the lead. I would be happy to buy that kind of lead anytime. More about how you can find these kinds of deals in the next chapter.

Don't worry about competition!

I sometimes hear about investors complaining that there is too much competition in the market for these below market value properties. Whilst I agree that there are apparently lots of investors looking for these deals, I would also argue that most of the investors in the market are amateurs and don't have the wherewithal to do these deals properly. It's not just about finding the deal. You need to be able to build a good relationship with the seller so that they work with you rather than your competition. I discovered that 1 wasn't the first investor to visit Bob in his home. While I was chatting with him, Bob told me that another company had been round to the property two weeks earlier but had not got back to him. I expressed my surprise at this and reassured Bob that if he worked with me, I would deal with his property sale in a fast and professional manner. I was able to build sufficient rapport with Bob such that he decided to work with me instead of the company that had been messing him around. It just goes to show that you need to be quick if you want to buy this kind of property. It is also vital that you are professional and ethical, but more on that in Chapter 4.

Alternative ways of funding your deals

Bridging finance

A method of buying property often used for its speed is bridging finance. This is an expensive way to purchase as the interest rate charged can be anything from 0.75% up to 2.5% per month and as such should only be used for short-term borrowing. The bridging company may lend up to 70% LTV and you have to put in the other 30% as a deposit. You would then look to refinance the property as soon as possible to reduce the cost of your borrowing. You may be able to borrow 100% of the purchase price if you can offer a second property with enough equity as security for the bridging company.

Although this way of buying is very expensive, the main reason people use bridging is because of the speed. Bridging can be arranged much faster than a traditional BTL mortgage. Very often it is used when buying properties at auction or in cases where you may not be able to obtain a traditional BTL mortgage. I have used bridging to be able to complete a purchase in as little as seven days, which is very fast, and thus buy at a very good price from someone who really needs to sell quickly.

Peer-to-peer lending

This is a new and innovative way to potentially fund your deals. From doing my own large development projects, I discovered how hard it can be to raise money with banks and I found that bridging can be expensive. I started to work with loans from private individuals with a minimum of £50k to invest who wanted to get a great return on their money while also looking over my shoulder to learn how I was managing these bigger projects.

This works really well for everyone involved, however I realised that many people would love to learn and earn at the same time but just don't have that kind of spare capital available. The way I was doing my developments meant I didn't want to take on projects with hundreds of people involved, as it could become a logistical nightmare. I decided the solution was to use technology to create a peer-to-peer lending platform where people could lend as little as £500 to experienced property developers and get a great return on their money, with the peace of mind that the platform would hold a first charge on the project on behalf of all the lenders. This means that in the unlikely event of a default by the borrower, CrowdProperty could take control of the property and manage it to ensure safe return of funds to the lenders.

I am delighted to announce that in 2014 we launched CrowdProperty which has since funded over £10m of development projects. Our primary objective is to make sure we look after our lenders and their money, so we only work with experienced developers whose projects are put through a strict due diligence process before they get the CrowdProperty stamp of approval and are listed on the platform.

If you want to understand how this works as either a lender or a borrower, then take a look at www.CrowdProperty.com. I believe this could become a mainstream method of funding property deals in the next few years.

Finding the deposit funds

Having enough money to put down as the deposit is one of the biggest challenges faced by most people who want to invest in property. Many people believe that you need to have lots of money sitting in the bank to be able to invest in property. That is simply not the case.

If you do have savings in the bank, then you should use that money first because it will be the cheapest way to fund your deposits. The profit you make each month from the positive cash flow on your investment properties should be much more than the interest you would otherwise earn if you just left the money in your bank account.

The average person does not usually have enough spare cash available to put down as a deposit, and so resigns themselves to the fact that they can't afford to get involved in property investing.

However, what many people do have is equity in property (often their own home), which can be released and used as deposits to buy more property. Many people don't like the idea of using equity from their own home to invest, as they are worried about the risks. Whilst I completely understand this natural concern, I would encourage you to have an open mind and think again. If you are going to use equity from your own home, you need to make sure you know what you're doing, and so it's highly fortuitous that you're educating yourself about how to successfully invest.

I would like to share with you a simple strategy for paying off your home mortgage and building a property portfolio in just eight to ten years. It's a very slow, but relatively safe strategy.

For the sake of this example, let's assume you've got some equity in your home. In fact, for many years you have been working hard to pay off your home mortgage. Please note that if you are only ever going to have one property (the home you live in), then it is a very good idea to pay off your home mortgage as quickly as you possibly can. By paying off your home mortgage you will be reducing one of your biggest outgoing expenses and you will reach financial independence far more quickly. However, investors think differently about this.

For most people, their home is the biggest asset they will ever own. Many people are content to pay off the mortgage, happy in the knowledge that, over time, the value of their asset will increase. If your home is worth £300,000 now, then you could just sit back and relax and in 10 years' time your property will probably double in value to £600,000. How would that make you feel?

Does this mean you are financially better off? Well, if your home is worth £600,000 you may feel much better than when it was worth £300,000. But in reality you are no better off. You see, all the other properties will also have gone up in value. If you wanted to move from your existing home to a similar sized property, in a similar area, then that would also cost you £600,000. In real terms you've had no net gain. And for you to benefit from that increase in value you would have to sell your home and downsize to a smaller, cheaper property or move to a more affordable area, which is what many people do when they retire.

Investors recognise that it's beneficial to have more than one property because they can profit from the increased capital value of their entire property portfolio, especially if they've used other people's money to buy that portfolio.

Consider this alternative strategy. Instead of trying to pay off their own home mortgage as quickly as possible, investors will do the opposite! They will use as much equity as they can from their existing properties to buy more to expand the portfolio.

Remember, in this example we are going to assume you've got £300,000 of equity in your own home and let's say you could release up to 80% of the value of that equity, which means that you would be able to release £240,000 to use as seed capital for your deposits.

To keep the example simple, we will assume the investment properties you would purchase are worth about £200,000 in today's market.

If you were to use 75% LTV mortgages, that means you could get a £150,000 BTL mortgage on each investment property and you would be required to put in a £50,000 deposit.

With seed capital of £240,000, you would have deposits for four investment properties (4 x £50,000 = £200,000) and you would have £40,000 left over to cover your purchasing costs such as Stamp Duty, solicitor's and surveyor's fees.

You would then be the proud owner of a property portfolio containing your own home (worth £300,000) and four investments at £800,000 (4 x £200,000) with a total value of £1.1m.

Don't forget that you will also have some debt! There is the £240k mortgage from your own home, and you also have four investment mortgages of £150k (4 x £150k = £600k), which means your total debt is £840k (£240k + £600k).

That might feel like a lot of debt and it might scare you, but the great thing is you are not going to be covering the cost of that debt. The tenants in your rental properties should be covering the cost of that borrowing.

Having done the initial hard work of finding and buying the right four properties, you sit back and wait! If property prices were to double on average in the next 10 years, your total portfolio would increase in value from £1.1m to £2.2m.

Your outstanding debt, which was taken out as interest-only mortgages, is still only £840k. That means you have a total of £1.36m of equity – that's quite a hefty lump of equity to have.

At some point in the future you would want to pay off the mortgage on your own home. Each of the investment properties would be worth £400k with an investment mortgage of just £150k. What you could do is re-mortgage some or all of those investment properties to take out, let's say, £60k from each property. That would give you £240k in cash which you could use to clear all of the debt on your own home, and you would still have the four investment properties giving you a rental income and almost £1m of equity in your investment portfolio.

So far we have just looked at 10 years from now. What if prices were to then double again in the following ten years? Now you can see how real wealth is created by the long-term buying and holding of property.

You might be thinking this all sounds great, but I don't have enough deposit to purchase four investment properties. Remember, as I explained earlier with Momentum Investing, you can quickly recycle your deposit. If you don't even have enough for one deposit, then there are lots of ways to use other people's money to build your property portfolio

Using other people's money to fund your deposits

If you don't have savings or any equity available in your own home, don't worry, as there are plenty of other ways to fund your deposits. You may well have some assets you could use to invest with that you are not aware of. That's why I have created the Hidden Assets Test which is one of the profile tests that I mention in Chapter 8.

Most successful investors use other people's money because no matter how much money you have, at some point you will run out of your own personal funds. I need to make it very clear that when using other people's money you need to be very careful and make sure you can return their money to them when agreed.

Asking other people to lend money to you can feel very awkward but it's all about the way you do it. Instead of feeling that you are begging other people for money or asking for help, you need to realise that, in fact, you are sharing an opportunity with them to make some money by giving them a better return on it than they currently receive. You need to be able to demonstrate that you know what you're doing and that their money is safe with you. There are always risks in lending money and so you need to minimise those risks for the private lender.

There are many different sources of deposit money you can access. Here are some ideas to stimulate your thinking:

Other people's savings: There will be people you know, who have money in the bank, to whom you can offer a higher return than they are currently receiving from their bank. With the Bank of England base rate having been so low for many years, it's possible to provide a much higher return than they are currently receiving.

Other people's equity: I am sure you have family and friends who have plenty of equity and may like to invest in property but have no idea how to do it. You could joint venture with them whereby you put in the time and effort and they provide the seed capital for deposits.

Inheritance in advance: Do you have any family from whom you will eventually inherit some money? Would it be possible to get some of that money in advance? If they give you some money and then live for at least another seven years, the gift would be considered to be outside of their estate and so would avoid any Inheritance Tax liability. The other benefit is that they see you prospering from their gift while they are still alive. We call this giving with warm hands!

Personal loans and credit cards: Where else could you borrow money from? Could you take out a private loan? I have even purchased property using credit card cheques for the deposit, although this is an advanced strategy and you need to be very careful that you have a clear exit strategy. I would not recommend this.

Retained Business Profits: Maybe you have a business that has retained profits. Rather than leaving the money in the business bank account, could you use a director's loan from your business and pay interest to your business for the loan. Who do you know who has a profitable business?

Pension money: In the past it has not been possible to use pension funds to purchase residential property without incurring a huge tax charge. However, since April 2015, people aged 55 and above have been able to access a tax-free lump sum from their pension savings, and as much as they wish during retirement, subject to their marginal rate of income tax. What this means is many people over the age of 55 with pensions might well be looking for ways of getting a better return than they traditionally receive from their pension. Maybe you could help them with that!

Other investors: Maybe you know some other investors with whom you can do joint ventures. If you get good at finding the deals, there should be no problem in finding people who will come into the project with you on a joint venture basis. You could achieve far more working with someone else's resources rather than having to work with just your own. We talk more about this in Chapter 7.

The seller: And finally, how about the seller of the property that you want to purchase? What are they going to do with the proceeds of the sale? If they are downsizing, do they need all of the money? If they are just going to put the money in their bank, then maybe you can give them a better return on their money.

There are many different ways to find the deposits. The key here is to remember that you want to use as little of your own money as possible so that you are not limited to the number of properties you can purchase.

The next step

Once you have sourced the deposit finance, you need to focus on finding motivated sellers who will either sell their property to you for less than the true market value or be flexible on the terms of the sale.

By purchasing at a significant discount (and adding value where possible), you should be able to use Momentum Investing to refinance the property quickly to pull out the deposit and use it on the next purchase, thus building a portfolio with No Money Left In (NMLI).

What could NMLI strategies do for you?

Using these strategies, there is no limit to the number of properties you can buy. All you need to do is find the motivated sellers, and the good news is there are motivated sellers everywhere. You just need to know where and how to find them and, more importantly, how to help them solve their problems which is exactly what we will cover in the next two chapters.

How many properties are you going to buy over the next 12 months?

The average property value in the UK is about £200,000. If you were to obtain a 25% discount on this value of property, you would get £50,000 of equity each time you bought a property.

If you bought one property a month, after 12 months you would have £2.4m worth of property with £600,000 of equity; that's very good, but let's consider what happens in 10 years' time when those properties may well have doubled in value. Your £2.4m of property will be worth something like £4.8m. The equity in your property portfolio will be worth £3m. Would that be enough money to support you and your family in your retirement?

Let me just clarify that all you would be doing is buying one property each month for 12 months. That's it! I am not talking about working for 10 years. I am talking about working smart for just one year, then you can sit back and wait while the value of your properties increases with time. If you put your mind to it, do you think you could do it?

There is a huge opportunity for you right now whilst most people are still thinking about it. So why wait? Now is the time to take action.

Chapter 3:

There are plenty of motivated sellers who will be flexible on price and / or terms of the sale

Why would someone sell their property below market value?

If you've ever sold a property, I am sure you probably wanted to achieve the highest possible sale price. It is hard to imagine why this is not the case for everyone selling property. However, it would be wrong to assume that everyone is like you. There are people who, for whatever reason, need to get their hands on money fast.

One of the disadvantages of property is that it is not a liquid asset. If you want to turn your asset into cash, generally it takes two to three months to complete a sale on a property, and that is once you've found a willing buyer. Even if you do find a buyer, there is no guarantee that the sale will go through. According to the Department of Trade and Industry, approximately one in three property sales falls through in the UK. This is a very important statistic, which could make you a lot of money as we will learn later.

Unfortunately, some people cannot afford to wait for two to three months to get the money from their property. They need the money now, or at least within a few weeks. For these motivated sellers, the speed and reliability of the sale is more important than the actual amount of cash they generate from the sale. If you're able to help these people to get the cash they need in the time that they need it, they may be prepared to sell you their property for less than it's worth. You need to put yourself in their shoes to try and understand the situation the seller may be in.

So let's consider some of the reasons why sellers could be motivated enough to be flexible on price or terms.

Repossession:

Many people in the UK are in debt. As well as their mortgages, they have personal loans and credit cards, and they simply cannot keep up with all the payments. The danger is that if they don't keep up their mortgage payments, their property may get repossessed and they will lose their home. If your property is repossessed, you get kicked out of your home, bringing public humiliation and embarrassment, ruining your credit rating and making it very difficult to get funding in the future. If the property is sold for less than it's worth, you probably won't get any of the equity from the sale. In fact, if the sale of the property doesn't generate enough money to cover your mortgage balance and all the costs, you may be pursued by the mortgage company for up to 12 years after the repossession.

Unfortunately, repossessions are on the increase in the UK. More and more people who find themselves in this position would prefer to sell their property below market value rather than have it repossessed. Although the seller will not get the full market value from their property, at least they get to clear their debts, their credit record remains relatively intact, and they have some chance of starting again.

Cash flow problems:

Occasionally you hear of perfectly good, successful and profitable companies that go out of business due to cash flow issues. Imagine the scenario where a successful business owner has, over the years, wisely reinvested the profit from their business back into residential property. However, in tough economic times maybe that business is now struggling and the business owner decides that they need to inject some cash into the business to save it. Selling some of their investment properties below market value to raise some cash quickly to support the business would be preferable to their business going bust!

Many amateur investors believe that motivated sellers are only people at the bottom end of the market. This is incorrect.

Wealthy people also have cash flow issues, which could be solved by selling some of their assets such as investment properties. In 2015, I had the good fortune to spend six days on Necker Island with a small group of entrepreneurs and Sir Richard Branson. Whilst we were on the island, he told us the story of how he purchased Necker in the late 1970's massively below market value. It was on the market for $6m but Sir Richard made an offer of $100,000 which not surprisingly was rejected. However the wealthy owner, Lord Coldham, did indeed sell the island to Sir Richard about a year later for just $180,000 because he had a short-term cash flow issue.

Downsizing:

This often occurs as people get older. Imagine a married couple who have been living in their good-sized home with their kids for a number of years. But maybe the kids have left home now and the two parents are rattling around in a large house. They decide to move to a smaller home or relocate to a warmer climate overseas where property may well be cheaper. If you were retiring and found your dream cottage or bungalow to retire to, you might decide that in order to secure your dream property, you have to sell your current home very quickly, and so selling at a discount could be preferable to losing out on your dream home.

Emigrating:

When people move overseas, they sometimes decide that they want to dispose of property in the UK because they don't want the hassle of looking after it or maintaining it when they are away. In addition to this, people may need to sell their UK property to build or purchase overseas. In this instance, sellers will often accept a price below the true market value if it means they can move quickly and fulfil their dreams overseas.

Accidental landlord:

Occasionally people become landlords by accident. They inherit a property or have a property that they don't sell and decide to rent it out instead. Being a landlord does have its challenges and you can understand how someone may become tired and fed up with being a landlord, and so look to sell their property just to get away from the hassle of renting it out, or the liability of the mortgage debt.

Broken chain:

With approximately one in three house sales in the UK falling through, it is no wonder that selling a property can be a very frustrating and upsetting procedure. Imagine if you were trying to sell your property and your buyer had pulled out, not just once but twice. You may be pretty motivated to sell your property, because otherwise you may feel you'll never get to sell and move on. Most people who have owned a property for a long time will have experienced some strong capital growth in their property, and may not need all the equity in the property in order to move on to the next one, especially if they are downsizing. Potentially, selling the property quickly for less than it's worth may be a good solution to allow them to move on and get on with their life.

Deceased estate:

Often when people inherit property, they don't know what to do with it. It may be located on the other side of the country. It may need work or maintenance, and it may be inherited by several different people. The beneficiaries may decide that selling the property is better than holding on to it, so they can all get some cash from the sale. Depending on personal circumstances, some of the beneficiaries may need money sooner than others, and so may be happy to sell the property for less than it is worth. After all, it has not cost them anything.

Divorce:

Unfortunately, 40% of marriages end in divorce these days. Sometimes things get a bit messy and the two partners just want to split as quickly as possible. The sale of the family home can often take a long time and cause unnecessary heartache. In this circumstance, the sellers may be prepared to sell the property for less than it is worth just so they can split the assets and get on with their separate lives.

Undesirable Property:

Sometimes property just doesn't seem to sell because it doesn't look appealing, needs too much doing to it, or could even be one of those 'Smelly Houses' – you know what I mean!

Maybe the property needs too much work doing to it so that it may not be eligible for a mortgage in its current condition. This would put off the majority of investors and so the property may remain on the market until it is offered at a price low enough to make the project viable.

The common theme

You may have noticed with all of the above reasons for being a motivated seller that there is a common theme. In all of the situations described, the seller had a property-related problem.

As a property entrepreneur, you are a property problem-solver. Solve someone's problem and you will get rewarded financially. It is your job to find out exactly what the problem is and work out a solution to the problem that works for you and the seller.

How to find motivated sellers

Most people who are selling property will want to achieve the highest possible price. Maybe only three or four people out of every 100 people selling their property will be motivated enough to give you the kind of discount you want. As a property problem-solver, you have to become good at finding motivated sellers. The good news for you is there are motivated sellers absolutely everywhere. All you have to do is find them.

There are many shrewd investors in the UK who realise that buying property below market value from motivated sellers is probably the best investing strategy, no matter what the current market conditions. This means that there is competition in the market. You need to make sure you stand out from the competition. There are two ways of doing this. Firstly, you need to make sure your marketing message is strong in order to get sellers to contact you; secondly, you need to make sure that the seller is persuaded to deal with you, rather than any other investor.

There are a number of different ways of finding motivated sellers. In this section we will briefly consider a number of strategies. To help bring these strategies to life for you, I have asked some of the delegates on my Property Mastermind Programme if they would provide some case studies of actual deals they have done. With their permission, some of the details of these deals are outlined throughout this book for your benefit, to help you understand the motivation of the sellers.

Estate agents

Not surprisingly, my very first property purchase was from an estate agent. I didn't realise there were any other ways of buying a property. It took me 11 years before I realised that I could get motivated sellers to come direct to me. If you want to buy a property, it makes sense to go and speak to someone who represents lots of sellers. You would think estate agents would be an excellent source of motivated sellers. After all, the estate agents will know when a sale has fallen through, or if the seller needs to sell in a particular hurry.

This is all good in theory, but I often hear investors complain that they cannot get any good deals from estate agents, because the estate agent has a shortlist of investors who they call first whenever they get a really good deal. Generally, this is true, and so many investors don't bother to look for motivated sellers at estate agents because they think the agents will give all the best deals to their friends.

Estate agents aren't stupid. If they have a good deal that they can sell by calling one person rather than having to show 10 people around the property, what do you think they would rather do? I can tell you right now, some of my best deals have come from estate agents. I have sometimes been told about properties that are for sale before the "For Sale" board goes up, and even before the agent has produced the sale particulars for the property. If one of the local agents with whom I work finds a property that suits my criteria, they will always call me first because they know if it is right for me, I will buy it. It saves them a lot of time and hassle, and it gives the seller a fast and certain solution to their problem.

As an investor, one of your goals should be to get on your local estate agent's shortlist (sometimes called their "little black book"), so that you are one of the people they call whenever they get a good deal. The mistake that most amateur investors make is that they walk into an estate agent and ask the agent for all their motivated sellers, explaining that they want to buy property 20% or more below market value.

In response to this, most estate agents will usually roll their eyes and think, "Here's another one, I've heard all this before! Another know-it-all, time-wasting investor!" As soon as the amateur investor leaves the office, their business card will be promptly put in the rubbish bin and the estate agent will never think of them again. It is no surprise that most investors struggle to get great deals from estate agents.

You need to understand how to speak to estate agents in such a way that they want to do business with you.

You need to demonstrate to the estate agent that:

- **You know what you're doing without sounding arrogant,** so that they feel you are asking them to help you because you see them as the expert. Even if you do know more than the estate agent, never let them know that.

- **You are a serious investor,** unlike all the other time-wasting, amateur investors.

- **You have money ready to invest** so that you can move as quickly as you say you can.

- **You act promptly, efficiently and professionally** which means that you are not going to mess them or their sellers around.

It can take a while to build a trusting relationship with estate agents, but if you put the effort in you should get good results. You need to keep in touch with them on a regular basis so that they remember you.

Instead of asking the estate agents directly if they have any motivated sellers, which may not get the response from the agent that you want, there are five specific questions you can use to identify the circumstances which might mean that the sellers are motivated.

Here are the 5 questions to ask estate agents:

1. Do you have any empty properties?

There are four main reasons why a property could be empty:

- If the property looks a bit trashed, it could be a repossessed property as often they are damaged on the way out by the previous owner who understandably could be bitter about the repossession.

- If it looks dated and in need of modernisation (often with some furniture left in it), it could be a deceased estate, as someone has probably lived there for many years and not made many recent improvements to the property.

- If it is in good condition but empty with no furniture, then it could well be that the seller has already moved to a new property whilst trying to sell this one.

- If it looks a bit tired and is being sold with some furniture in it, then it may well be a former rental property that a landlord is selling.

In all four cases, as the property is sitting there empty, the seller could be motivated to sell at a good price.

2. Do you have any property that has been on the market a long time?

This question will identify properties that are just not selling. Maybe the price is too high or something about the property is putting off potential buyers. It may well be that a sale had been agreed and has fallen through on the property, which might make the seller even more frustrated.

In any case, maybe there is some scope for a discounted offer. You can track changes in property prices by using websites like www.property-bee.com.

3. Do you have any properties where there is more than one agent selling it?

Often sellers will list their property with two agents or more in an attempt to find a buyer quickly. They may not be willing to sell at the price you are prepared to pay, but it is certainly worth a look. The agent may be worried that they will not earn any commission if the other agent finds a buyer and so they may be more motivated to work with you to find a win/win for the vendor and you.

4. Do you have any properties that are listed for sale or for rent?

You often find that people are keen to sell their property, but will consider renting for a while if they are unable to sell. This is perfect for you if you are looking for Purchase Lease

Options, whereby you rent out the property with the right to buy in the future. You would normally pay the estate agent their fee at the time you sign the contracts, otherwise they will not get paid until the end of the option period – which could be several years – so this may not be very popular with some agents. Remember, the agents need to see what is in it for them and the seller, if you want them to agree to anything slightly different from the norm. We will look at this strategy in depth in Chapter 6.

5. Do you have any sellers who keep calling the office to see if there is any news on their sale?

This is a sure sign that the seller is getting desperate; every few days they call the estate agent to see if there is any news. Often the seller will not tell the agent the full details of their situation, but this behaviour is a sure sign that they are anxious to sell and so there may be a deal there. This person may be starting to annoy the staff in the agency, so when you ask this particular question, often a specific seller will spring to mind!

What to do when you get a lead

Once an agent gives you a lead you need to act quickly. First of all, you need to find out from the estate agent as much information as possible about the property, the seller and their circumstances. Very often the agent may not have the information that you would normally get from the seller, so you need to arrange a visit to the property when the seller is there if at all possible.

That means usually asking for a viewing in the evening or at the weekend, outside the normal estate agency working hours. You are not attempting to cut the agent out in any way, but it is always best, if you can speak to the seller direct, to find out what is truly important to them. Remember, if the seller is genuinely motivated, it is not always the highest offer they go for, but the need for speed and certainty. If you do meet the seller in person, ask them for their contact details in case you have any further questions.

Always give feedback to the estate agent about the viewing and share your thoughts. If you have made an offer to the seller, always pass it through the agent as well, to make sure they don't think you are trying to cut them out of the deal. If the offer is not accepted, tell them that you will leave it on the table and make sure you follow up every few weeks, to see if the seller has become more motivated so that they will now consider your offer.

Once you have successfully completed a purchase through an estate agent, you need to go straight back to them and tell them that you are looking for another purchase. As you have just demonstrated that you are a serious investor, they will take you far more seriously than other investors interested in the same kind of deals. You will have worked your way onto their shortlist of preferred investors they call whenever they get a good deal.

Case Study: Rob and Nicola McPhun

I am retired from the police after 34 years of service and our reason for investing in property was to help my wife Nicola replace her income as she was still working as a police officer.

Having established a close professional relationship with a local estate agent in Hull, he rang me one day to ask if I would be interested in buying an unlicensed House of Multiple Occupation which he had been asked to sell but was not listed yet. He was going down to measure up and take photos of the property for the website, etc, and offered me the chance to have a look before anyone else. Of course I accepted his invitation and agreed to meet him at the property.

The property was a three-storey Victorian terraced house, which was being used as an unlicensed 11-bedroom HMO for Local Housing Authority residents. There had been lots of issues with it, including its use for drugs and parties, etc. Showing the estate agent round was the current letting agent. I made enquiries with him as to who the owner was so I could speak to them personally. The owner was an absent landlord who had been previously using his cousin as the letting agent, but he was well known in the town as being of rather dubious character which had led to the Council's HMO officer serving a notice on the owner to bring the premises up to standard. I subsequently contacted the owner and they asked for £120k stating they had bought it and spent £30k refurbishing it. They had no mortgage on the property. We could see based on room size that it had potential to be a good sized licensed HMO with eight bedrooms. Based on that we offered £90k which was refused outright. That was in December, and so we put the lead into our follow-up system as we were taught to do.

In our January Property Mastermind Workshop we were reminded of the importance and simplicity of following up all the properties we had made offers on. So I called the seller on my drive back home and he asked me if my offer of £90k still stood as they had experienced further issues with the property and wanted to get rid of it. I said yes, but due to his delay in accepting our initial offer we had used our cash as a deposit on a freehold building of three flats and I would get back to him regarding ways to buy. The owner definitely wanted to sell as they wished to invest the money in a BTL although they were in no hurry as they had not sourced one yet.

After some negotiation we settled on an exchange with delayed completion, whereby we put down a £5k deposit with three months to completion. It turned out that this was too ambitious in terms of getting a licence and the work needed to reach that standard. So, two months in, we re-negotiated the completion date for another seven months, which allowed us to refurb and tenant the property before completion. We spent £23k on the refurb (electric/ fire alarms upgrade, plumbing and redecoration being the main costs). In the end, one room was 2 sq ft undersized due to head height (sloping ceiling) and the HMO officer only granted seven-bedroom status. Following this, the RICS Valuation based on a seven-bedroom HMO was £135K subject to planning.

A summary of the deal is as follows:

- Property sourced through a local estate agent
- Purchase price £90k, with a £5k deposit and nine months delay until completion. Mortgage 75% LTV meaning a loan of £62.5k
- Refurb costs £23k
- Monthly mortgage costs of £313 with all other bills of £493 means total monthly costs of £806
- Rented out as a seven-bed licensed HMO with a monthly income of £2,489
- Total monthly profit of £1,683, which is an ROI of 40.3%

Following Planning Permission approval, we anticipate refinancing up to that valuation and getting £101k back with £23k left in. We will then re-mortgage the property at an LTV of 75%, which will release £38k to reinvest in another property. Our cash flow will reduce by about £300pcm due to higher monthly mortgage costs and our ROI will be 138.6%.

I am delighted that since starting our Property Mastermind journey we have purchased five more properties using our own and other people's money, with the result of £3,087 net passive income per month, and Nicola has been able to retire early from the police force.

Auctions

You would think that an auction would be a great place to pick up a bargain property and yes, that can be the case. However, the reality is that often investors end up paying too much for a property because they get carried away in the bidding due to a lot of competition in the room. The job of the auctioneer is to squeeze as much money as they can out of the room for each property they sell.

It is possible to get a good deal from motivated sellers through auctions but there is a specific way to do it which does not involve bidding in the room on the day of the auction. I will explain this Auction Purchasing Strategy, but first there are a few things you need to understand about auctions.

Generally, sellers put properties into auctions for a number of reasons:

They need to sell fast: If the property is sold in the room, then the buyer will exchange that day and needs to complete 28 days after exchange. This gives certainty to the owner who knows they will get paid very quickly.

The property is a dog: This means that there is something wrong with the property. Maybe there is a structural issue, or perhaps it's not possible to get a mortgage on it, so the seller puts it into the auction in the hope that someone who does not know what they are doing will buy it. Once they have exchanged the buyer has committed, and many amateurs end up getting caught out buying this way.

They want to get top sales price: Some property traders deliberately sell their properties at auctions because they expect the potential buyers to keep bidding against each other until someone buys the property for more than it is really worth. See the Dave Guest case study in Chapter 5 about selling a property in auction.

Six tips for buying at auction

If you are going to buy at auction, there are a few things you need to know to ensure that you don't make an expensive mistake:

1. Properties are often listed at a low guide price to generate interest from many potential buyers but will only be sold if the price goes above the reserve price set by the seller.

2. Do your own due diligence and make sure you understand what you are buying and how much it will cost to fix it up.

3. Always get a solicitor to check the legal pack for the property on your behalf, before the auction, to make sure that everything is in order and that you are happy to exchange on the day, if indeed you are the successful bidder.

4. Make sure you have your finance in place, as you will need 10% on the day of the auction to exchange and then the balance 28 days later. That is not enough time to arrange a normal mortgage and so you will probably need bridging finance which will cost you more.

5. Work out the maximum price you are prepared to pay, and if bidding goes beyond that price, make sure you sit on your hands. Don't be tempted to pay any extra over the maximum price you have set.

6. Be prepared to walk away from the property if it goes for more than you are prepared to pay, even if you have spent money on legal fees and surveys, etc.

Auction Purchase Strategy

There are actually three different occasions when you can buy a property that is listed for sale by auction. These are: on the day itself, which is what most people do; before the auction actually happens; or after the auction, if bidding fails to hit the reserve price.

I believe you can sometimes get the best deals after the auction when the property has failed to reach the reserve price. The seller who thought they would have their money 28 days after the auction may well be strongly motivated given that it failed to sell, and there may be a deal that can work for everyone.

After the auction you can approach the auctioneer and see if there is room for negotiation. Even better, if you can talk to the seller direct and establish what their motivation is, you can try to solve their problem with an ethical win/win solution.

In Chapter 6, you can read an interesting case study from Dave Morris who picked up a fantastic property that failed to sell at auction.

Newspaper adverts

If you pick up a copy of your local free newspaper and look in the classified section, you will often find adverts from buyers who are offering to purchase property for cash with fast completion. Depending on where you live, there may be lots of buyers advertising in this way. The reason they are advertising there is because it works; if it didn't, they wouldn't be doing it week in, week out. Some of the buyers advertising are national companies but many of them will be local investors just like you and me.

Sometimes, the investors I work with often feel it's not worth advertising in newspapers because of all the competition. I will acknowledge that yes, there may be lots of buyers advertising in your local newspaper, but I would put money on the fact that at least half of them don't really know what they're doing. A lot of people will see someone else using a certain strategy and try to copy it, without really understanding it. I have called many buyers advertising in newspapers, just to check out the competition. I am shocked at how amateurish most of the people are who answer the phone and how ineffective they are at asking the right questions. So yes, there are other investors advertising but I don't see them as competition, and nor should you, as long as you know what you're doing.

You will need to run your newspaper advert every week over several months to get some reasonable responses. Don't expect to place the advert just once and get flooded by calls. If you get a call from a motivated seller who has seen your advert, there is a good chance they will also have called some of the other advertisers as well. You need to be really good at building rapport on the telephone and moving very quickly to take advantage of the deal, otherwise your competition will beat you to it.

Copywriting guidelines

People have written entire books about copywriting, but I want to give you a really quick lesson in how to get a better response from your adverts.

There are three key components to any advert: The Headline, The Body Copy and The Call to Action.

The Headline: This has to grab the attention of the reader, make them stop and want to read more about your product or service. Decide what type of seller you are aiming to attract.

The Body Copy: This is where you promote the benefits of your service. This should explain what's in it for the reader! You need to target your message to appeal to the reader.

The Call to Action: This is where you tell the reader what you want them to do next, e.g. to call you now on a certain number.

What do you want them to do if they are interested in your service?

Case Study: Dean and Mandy Purkiss

Dean and I started to invest five years before we joined the Property Mastermind Programme, and in that time we managed to purchase eight investment properties, until we ran out of deposit money. We then heard about the Property Mastermind Programme and realised that we did not have to use our money to build our cash-flow-generating property portfolio.

On the Property Mastermind Programme we were taught many different strategies for lead generation and we found that newspaper advertising was by far the best response in our area.

One day we received a message from our call answering service to say that Mrs X had phoned and seemed somewhat annoyed that we had not called her back. This was initially confusing because we ensure we always call people back when we say we will, and also we did not recognise her name or address!

Dean telephoned Mrs X and discovered she had in fact spoken to another investor who advertises in the same newspaper, who had not got round to calling her back!

Dean then asked about her situation and discovered that her reason for selling was due to her ill health and her desire to move into a smaller property because she had lost her husband.

Dean thought we could probably help her and arranged for me to visit the property and sit down with Mrs X to find a win/win solution.

Prior to visiting the property, I did my research and found the property was already being advertised by an estate agent at a significantly reduced price of £115k. Similar properties on the same street were being marketed at £160k to £170k. I also checked the previous sold prices in the area and this confirmed that the property was greatly reduced.

When I met with Mrs X at the property, she explained she had already found somewhere much smaller that she wanted to move to, but needed to sell her property first. She said that she wanted to be able to sell quickly to move on and have some 'pension' money in her bank account. She was struggling to stay on top of the cleaning in the house and found, due to her health, that it was extremely difficult climbing the stairs. She had contacted another investor in the paper who was supposed to get back to her, but after a week she had not heard from them. I assured her this would definitely not happen with us and so she was happy to move forward with the deal we had agreed.

I noticed several positive things while I was viewing the property. It had three double bedrooms and a separate downstairs dining room so it was perfect for a multi-let. The location was ideal, as it was extremely close to the town centre and the property required no work.

After building a rapport with Mrs X and finding out what she needed, we agreed on a purchase price of £85k. This enabled her to move on to a property much better suited to her needs. The sale progressed within six weeks and during that time we kept Mrs X updated on the situation and everything progressed smoothly.

Summary of this deal is as follows:

- This deal came as a direct result of our local newspaper advert.
- True market value of the property £160k with an agreed purchase price of £85k (47% BMV).
- We obtained a 75% BTL mortgage and used other people's money for the deposit.
- Six months later the property was re-mortgaged to remove all of the deposit and so there is now no money left in the property.
- Let out as a multi-let property this makes £650 positive cash flow each month after all bills and expenses.
- There is £75k equity left in the property.

This is just one of the 16 extra properties we have purchased in our 12 months on the Property Mastermind and we have also sourced and sold a further 87 properties for other investors, which has made us over £80k. We also now have a passive rental income of £7,500 per month, which means we have now both been able to give up full-time work and spend far more quality time with our kids. We love working in our property business and helping people solve their property problems.

Postcards

Postcards are an incredibly easy, cost-effective method of finding motivated sellers. However, many people overlook this method because it almost seems too simple. Investors don't believe that it would work, but it does. The basic idea is you create a small advert which you can place in the window of local corner shops or newsagents for a minimal cost each week. The copy on the postcard adverts would be very similar to that of a newspaper advert or leaflet. It just happens to be the same advert on show in one location for months and months on end. This method may not generate a lot of leads for you, but it does work as long as you have enough postcards in different shops. Don't be surprised if you don't get any response from the two postcards you have displayed, as that is not enough. Ideally you want hundreds of postcards all over the areas in which you invest.

The person who taught me about purchasing property below market value is an investor called David Price, from Leeds. One of David's main strategies for finding motivated sellers in his target area is through the use of postcards. David has about 250 postcards distributed throughout his area which generate approximately 10 enquiries a month, which translate into about one monthly deal.

Leafleting

The idea behind the leafleting strategy is that you can target specific areas in which you would like to buy below market value properties. You design a leaflet which explains the service that you provide to the seller, and then have it delivered to 15,000 to 20,000 households in your target area. To achieve good results, you do need to deliver high numbers of leaflets, but the benefit of this strategy is that you are going direct to the seller, and thus may have less competition than if they were to respond to an advert in a newspaper.

This strategy requires some capital input to pay for printing and distribution of your leaflets, plus it does take some time and effort to coordinate. But the results can be well worth the time and effort required.

It is not a good use of your time to distribute these leaflets yourself. You can either pay Royal Mail to do it for you or recruit your own team of leaflet distributors. Running your own team does take some effort and you need to put checks in place to ensure people are doing what they are supposed to do.

I do not recommend you put your leaflets in with the local free newspaper; the response rate will fall dramatically as most people put these leaflets straight in the bin.

Websites

One of the quickest and easiest ways to attract motivated sellers is through the internet. However, on the web you will face a lot of competition from other property problem-solvers. If a motivated seller completes an application form on your website, you can bet they have filled in applications on a number of other websites as well. Often it's the first property problem solver to contact the seller who'll secure the deal, as long as that investor knows what they are doing. Speed, as always, is critical here.

Developers and builders

It is possible to buy properties at a discount direct from developers and house builders at three specific times:

1. Off Plan, at the very beginning of a development, sometimes before they have started any work. This is when the builders will sell some units at a discount just to get some sales under their belt, which can help give confidence to the bank that is financing the development.

2. At the very end of a development, when there are just a few units left unsold and the builder wants to sell the last few so they can shut the showroom and move on to the next development.

3. If the builder is a big PLC house contractor, then you can sometimes get some great discounts towards the end of the financial year – especially if they have not quite achieved the sales targets they need to hit

to keep their shareholders happy. I have been able to attain some great discounts in the past by using this strategy.

There are many benefits to purchasing a brand new property such as low maintenance, etc, but just a word of caution here – be aware that new build is often priced at a premium because it is new, so make sure any discount you get is a genuine discount compared to other properties on the market.

And finally, it's worth mentioning that house builders will often accept other older properties as part exchange in order to sell their new properties. The builders have no interest in holding onto these part exchange properties and so just sell them on as quickly as possible to release their profits from these properties. You could pick up some good deals by purchasing part-exchange properties from builders at a discount.

Buying from other organisations

Very often companies, charities, organisations and councils have properties that they no longer need and decide to sell. Like the builders mentioned on the previous pages, these organisations are sometimes under pressure to sell within certain time frames for accounting reasons.

In 2013, I purchased a 10,000 sq ft commercial building from the council in Redcar which is on the north-east coast of England. They had been trying to sell their former youth centre for a while but had been unable to get the price they wanted. However, the council had to sell the property before the end of their financial year and they were running out of time.

We agreed a sale and completed in two weeks to help them achieve their timescale which was most important to them. We were able to purchase this large building for £250,000. We then spent £400,000 creating 20 units which are a mixture of one-and two-bedroom apartments. These affordable units are worth at least £50k each, which, with the freehold, values the development at about £1.1m. We have now refinanced the building to repay all of the private lenders and have an apartment block with £400k of equity and no money left in, and which now generates £4k of profit each month when fully tenanted.

So the question for you is – are there any empty buildings in your area owned by companies or organisations which may want to dispose of these assets? You can go on the Land Registry website, find out who owns them and then approach the owner to see if they are interested in selling.

CASE STUDY:
Tim and Klare Percival

My wife and I live in Bristol and we were both doctors working as full-time General Practitioners for the NHS.

We were extremely stressed and wondered what life was all about. We were the stereotypical professionals who didn't have any quality of life because we worked such long and busy hours. Something had to change.

Then in 2014 I read this book, *Property Magic*, and suddenly I realised that there was an alternative to what we were doing. I wanted my life to change rapidly and I knew I needed to learn some new skills, so I joined the Property Mastermind Programme.

Whilst on Mastermind, our lives did change very quickly. The deal we are about to share is what we affectionately call a 'retire in 1 deal' property and the favourite in our portfolio for many reasons.

Ever since we settled in Bristol we wanted to own one of an historic parade of houses lying just below the famous Clifton Suspension Bridge. They are among the oldest houses in Bristol, dating from the mid 1700s. They are 5-storey, grand, Grade 2-listed beauties. So many times I drove past and wondered... never believing I could own one of them. Even more, I couldn't believe I could make profit out of one. Each time I drove by I noticed a student-let sign of a well-known student letting company in Bristol. (I work as a GP at the University of Bristol, so had walked past the houses on my way for lunch for the previous five years!).

In the end, I did some research into the property, and through the council HMO landlord database found out that it was a massive 16-bedroom licensed HMO, owned by a student housing company based in the Midlands. This was their only property in Bristol and all their other properties were in cities in the Midlands or South Wales. We wrote them a letter asking if they were interested in selling. Amazingly they were. In fact, by luck, the previous week they had decided at a company review meeting that this house was a bit out of the way for them and they were considering a sale. Our letter arrived with perfect timing.

On viewing the property, we found it needed a refurbishment in the not-too-distant future but was still in average condition. What was obvious to us was that the level of rent they were getting was way below the standard rent achieved in Bristol. The company clearly didn't know the Bristol market well enough and were basing their prices on the rents achieved further north. The other huge positive was that the house was already licensed, and also already had planning for being a large HMO which was important as it was in the Article 4 part of Bristol.

We managed to negotiate an off-market purchase. We got on very well with the previous owners and continue to be in contact. The amazing part was that to add value to this property we spent nothing on the house. We just increased the rents by £3k per month to the local going rate. Our local expertise enabled us to spot this deal and easily add value.

Summary of deal:

- Purchase price £720k
- Refurb costs £0
- Interest on 75% Commercial Mortgage @5.5%. = £2,310 pcm
- Cost of bills and extras £1,000 pcm
- Total costs inc. mortgage £3,310 pcm
- Rental income £8,500 pcm (previous rental income £5,500 pcm)
- Profit monthly £5,190 pcm
- Annual profit £62,280
- Money Left in £243,500
- Return on Investment 26%

As this was a very big deal, it may not have been a good one for a first deal but in fact was our 5th deal whilst on Mastermind, so we had already learnt exactly how to deal with a big property like this. The profit on this one property could make two average earners in the UK financially free. We now have a large portfolio and have a passive income, which means we can choose how we spend our time. Interestingly, we still choose to do some NHS GP work and now enjoy it, as we do a small amount on our terms. Property-wise we are moving more into larger developments including a current 10-house heritage development south of Bristol.

The Property Mastermind Programme has totally changed our life for the better. Don't underestimate what can be achieved in a small amount of time when you have a strong enough reason why, as well as the drive and commitment to succeed.

Buying leads from other investors

If you don't want to set up your own lead-generating systems, you may decide that the easier route for you to find motivated sellers is buying leads from other investors. I have found some fantastic investment opportunities which have come from other investors, like the one I described in Chapter 2, for which I paid the investor a finder's fee.

CASE STUDY: Tony Law

I'm a property investor based in Bournemouth and over the years I have bought and sold my fair share of properties. My strategy has always been to buy, refurbish and sell on – hopefully at a profit, although I would have to hold my hand up and say this hasn't always been the case.

Early in 2010, I read Simon's book, *Property Magic*, and although the book was laid out well and gave clear guidance on the techniques necessary to become successful in property, I would have to say there was one element in it that I really struggled with. This was the idea that it was possible to genuinely buy property at below market value. After all, why would anyone (in their right mind) sell their property at anything other than the full market value? It just didn't make any sense!

Some months later I heard there was a property investing event being held at the Excel centre in London and I knew Simon would be there, so I took it upon myself to confront him. This may sound dramatic, but I confess I was genuinely annoyed – if that isn't too strong a word – that it was even possible that anyone would openly suggest buying a property at anything other than the true market value.

Anyway, after spending a bit of time wandering around, talking to the other exhibitors, I had the opportunity to approach Simon on his stand and I asked my question. "Simon", I said, "I have been in property for a number of years. I understand you can get a better deal by seeking out motivated sellers, however I don't believe it is actually possible to buy a property at anything like 25% below market value in my neck of the woods." I will never forget Simon's answer. It was certainly not the answer I was expecting and it completely threw me. He asked me where I lived and then replied, "That explains it! You are absolutely right; Bournemouth is the only area in the UK where there has never been a repossession!"

This unexpected answer made me realise that maybe I had not looked at it from the motivated seller's point of view.

Following our conversation, I decided that I probably needed to open my mind up to the possibility that, maybe under certain circumstances, some people would sell their property for less than it is worth.

I decided to invest in my education and signed up for my wife and myself to attend Simon's one-day Mastermind Foundation quick start seminar.

One day with Simon answered many of my questions, and changed my mindset, such that within a month I had found my first, true, motivated-seller lead in my area which I purchased from another investor over the internet for just £49.

The property in question was a three-bedroom semi-detached house in Parkstone, Poole. Although externally the house was fine, to be honest internally this house was pretty awful. There was dirt, junk and even animal "deposits" everywhere, although I have to say the owners themselves were lovely people. They had a strong desire to move back to South Wales, and since the husband was disabled, houses suitable for the husband's needs did not come up very often. Since their own house was obviously going to prove difficult to sell and since suitable houses to buy in Wales came up pretty infrequently, they decided to sell their house at a discount to put them in a much stronger position to buy when the right house did come up – just so long as I was willing to accept a delayed completion – which I was happy to do.

As it happens, their ideal house turned up shortly after we agreed the deal and so the transaction was carried through conventionally.

Despite some very convincing comparables ranging from between £155k and £175k, I managed to negotiate a purchase price of £110k. The property did need a bit of work, however, which cost me a further £16k – so all in all, my BMV deal, with costs, came to £126k. Four months later the property was re-valued at £165k which I still feel is too cheap, but since this house is now bringing in £895.00 per month, I have no intention of selling it anyway.

Summary of this deal:

- I purchased this motivated seller lead for £49 from another investor
- Property worth £165k was purchased for £110k
- £16k of renovation was required so true purchase price is £126k
- Re-mortgaged to £123,750 (75% LTV) so less than £3k left in the property with over £40k equity in the property
- Rental income is £895 per month which after all expenses leaves a positive cash flow of £250 per month.

So, do I now believe it is possible to buy below market value in Bournemouth – you better believe it! And that was the problem before – because I did not believe it, I was looking for evidence to prove myself right. Now that I know that it can be done I am actively looking for more deals.

There are two main ways of finding leads from other investors:

The internet: There are several websites which specialise in attracting motivated sellers and then sell the leads on to other property problem-solvers. This can be a very quick and easy way to find deals. However, you need to be prepared to work through a number of leads which may not be suitable until you find a good deal. You also have to be quick as there may be many other investors using this route to find leads.

Networking: This is by far the best way – finding leads from other investors by getting to know them and building trusted working relationships. You can get to a position where other people are finding deals and bringing them to you for a finder's fee. The benefit of this over the internet is that you may have exclusivity on deals offered to you. A great place to meet property finders can be at the property investor network meetings all round the UK. On my Property Mastermind, we have an online forum where Mastermind members can share deals with each other. There is a high level of trust within my Property Mastermind group, with people working ethically together.

You must be ethical

When some people hear about the way we buy property below market value they question the ethics behind our motives. Some people may think that we're taking advantage of people in a vulnerable position, and I can see how it might look like that at first. I'm sure there are investors out there who do take advantage of motivated sellers, but this is not my style. I believe that if I approach the deal ethically, and if I am open and honest with the seller and find a true win/win deal that could help them and me, I am offering a service and providing a solution to their problem.

I'm about to give you probably the most valuable piece of information with regard to buying properties below market value. Are you ready for this? The most important piece of advice I would give any investor who is looking to buy proper market value from a motivated seller is this:

Whenever you meet a motivated seller, always hold their best interests at heart. You should constantly ask yourself the question, "How can I help this person?" If you come at this from the direction of trying to help people, you will stand head and shoulders above the rest of the competition. Before I buy a property from anybody, I make sure that selling their property to me really is their best option. This is so important that I am going to spend a whole chapter focusing on ethics and dealing with motivated sellers.

Before you move on to the next chapter, I invite you to re-read the paragraph above to make sure you really understand it. I cannot emphasise enough how important it is to genuinely want to help the seller. Put their interests first and you will end up doing more deals.

Chapter 4:

You should buy property ethically for a WIN/WIN solution

Dealing with motivated sellers

I am constantly amazed at the number of investors I meet who appeared to stumble across motivated sellers but who have no idea how to deal with them. If you want the motivated seller to work with you, rather than another investor, you need to make sure that they are confident that you can deliver on your promise. You need to ensure that you provide a prompt, professional and courteous service from the initial contact right up to completion of the purchase.

The first thing you need to consider is the initial point of contact. So, let's say you have an advert in the local newspaper, or have built your relationship with estate agents, or carried out your first leaflet campaign. What happens when your first motivated seller calls you? Do you know what to say to them? Do you know what information you need to gain from them? Do you know how to build rapport with them? If you don't make the right first impression, or even worse you expect them to leave their details on your answerphone, they will just call the next person advertising in the newspaper.

You have to be there, ready to take their call. If you can't be there because maybe you still work full time, delegate this to someone else. Do you know someone who could answer the phone for you? If not, maybe you should use one of those 24-hour answering services which will take the caller's details at any time of the day and send you a message by email, text or whatever is the most convenient format for you.

Whenever a motivated seller contacts you, you need to be quick. Remember, their whole motivation is around speed, so time is very valuable to them. There are certain key pieces of information which you need to acquire from the motivated seller to assess if this is a suitable deal for you or not.

Details you need to get from the seller:

- Their name and contact details, preferably a mobile telephone number

- The full address and postcode of the property they want to sell

- Is the property freehold or leasehold? If leasehold, how long is left on the lease and what are the service charges?

- A full description of the property, including:

  > Style of property, e.g. terraced, semi, detached, bungalow or flat

  > Number of bedrooms, bathrooms and living rooms

  > Who is living in the property

  > Does the property have double glazing, central heating, extensions or garage?

  > Has any work been done to the property, such as new kitchen, bathroom, etc?

- The reason why they are selling the property

- Their estimated valuation of the property and reasons to justify their estimate

- Are there any other investors interested?

- The particular timescales to which they are working

- When would be a good time to come and view the property?

These basic details will enable you to do your initial research to assess if there is a deal or not. Armed with this information, a few selected websites and a telephone, within about 20 minutes you can assess the opportunity to see if it is right for you.

You need to build a good rapport with the seller to get them to give you this information. It's no good rushing in, asking them how much they need and telling them you will only pay less than it is worth until you have a chance to explain what you do and put them at ease that they're dealing with a professional. You need to reassure the seller that your conversation is in complete confidence. You need to understand the seller's situation and try to put yourself in their shoes and understand how they will be feeling. They need a solution to their problem, and they need it quickly. That is why they are prepared to sell their house for less than it is worth.

Many investors feel that they can win a deal by outbidding the competition. This is not always the case. A few years ago I went to visit a motivated seller in Derby. We'll call her Sarah. Sarah and her husband wanted to sell their house so they could move on to a new property. The property was listed with an estate agent, and they had already had one sale fall through. They had no confidence in the estate agent and decided to try and sell the property privately, which is why they contacted me. While I was at the property, building rapport with Sarah, I found out that she had also contacted two other companies. The first company she spoke to was very impersonal on the phone and she didn't like them. The second company had been to visit her and had made her an offer.

Based on my research, I estimated the property was worth about £160,000. I calculated that I could offer Sarah £130,000 for the property. I had built a really good rapport with Sarah, and she told me that the other company had actually offered her more money, but she said that if I could match the offer, she would sell the property to me. I said I would go back to the office and look at my numbers again to see if I could increase my offer. I liked Sarah and I really wanted to help her. I thought about increasing my offer to £132,000 but it just wouldn't work for me. So I phoned Sarah about an hour later and explained that I was really sorry, but based on my figures, I could only offer her £130,000. I said that I was sorry I couldn't help and I recommended she should take the higher offer, which I believe was about £134,000. Sarah said that was a real shame, and she really wanted to deal with me because she trusted me. Thirty minutes later I had a phone call from Sarah who said she had just spoken to her husband and they had agreed to accept my offer and sell to me for £130,000. So the person who offers the most money does not always get the property; it is all about the relationship you develop with the seller.

Is everybody ethical?

There was a lot of negative media coverage in the press towards the end of 2007 regarding investors who were apparently ripping off desperate sellers, particularly when it came to Sale and Rent Back, which is why the FSA introduced the SARB requirements in July 2009.

Due to this negative press, some sellers (and their friends and family) can sometimes be sceptical of your motives. I am very upfront with sellers to whom I speak. I explain that I am not a charity and that I want to make money from any deal that we agree but it is also important for me to make sure that we find a win/win solution to their problem so that they are happy.

Everyone is better off with a win/ win deal

When you start advertising for motivated sellers you will no doubt speak to some people who are desperate to sell their property. However, there is absolutely no need to take advantage of these sellers. After all, you want to sleep at night with a clear conscience. I believe that if you find a win/win deal, you are genuinely helping the seller and providing a solution to their problem.

Remember the question at the end of the last chapter, "How can I help this person solve their problem?" The best way to do this is to ask the seller what they want. Find out what is really important to them and see if you can give them what they need. When I agree to buy property, the price I agree is the amount the seller will actually receive. There are no hidden fees or charges and I sometimes offer to cover the cost of their solicitor. If the seller is in debt, I only want to buy the property if I can help them to clear all of their debts with the proceeds from the sale of their property. I always find out how much they owe in total. Sometimes they are in so much debt that I just can't help them, in which case I might refer them to a reputable debt management company who may be able to help them.

Don't mess people around

It can be extremely stressful for a vendor trying to find someone to buy their property. If the individual needs to sell by a certain time, it can be even worse. It is really important that you as a potential buyer don't give the vendor false hope. Don't tell someone you can purchase their property if you have no intention of doing so. These people don't have a lot of time so you cannot afford to waste it. You need to be quick and decisive. If you can't help them, tell them, so they can move on and find another buyer. If you can help them, make sure you stick to your word. You need to give the seller certainty that you will do what you say you will do, when you say you will do it. I recommend you keep a diary and use it to schedule the time when you need to call the seller to keep them updated on progress of the sale of their property.

Communication is really important. Keep in touch with the seller throughout the process to let them know what is happening at every stage of the transaction. Remember the selling and buying process is probably a lot more stressful for the seller than it is for you. I learnt this the hard way.

When I first started to buy property this way, I lost a deal because I did not keep the seller updated as to what was happening. I agreed the purchase on a property in Birmingham on a Tuesday morning and said I would call the seller 'later'. What I meant by this was that I would call when I had some news. The seller thought I meant later that day! In her mind, when I didn't call when I said I would, she thought I had lost interest and so called another investor.

I had not wanted to call her until I had some positive news on the progress of the sale. So when I finally called on the Thursday morning with the news that the surveyor would be coming round the following day, she was rather surprised to hear from me and said that she had agreed a deal with someone else.

My poor communication had just caused me to lose a deal worth £20,000 in equity. Needless to say, I have not made that mistake again and I don't want you to make the same costly mistake either. Find out the expectations of the seller in terms of how often they want to hear from you, and make sure you keep the rapport going.

The Motivated Seller code of ethics

Along with several members of my Property Mastermind Programme, we have created a code of ethics, as outlined below, and I insist that everybody on my Programme follows it. Many of my investors actually show this code of ethics to potential sellers to reassure them that they are going to serve the seller as best they can.

- Any information disclosed to me by the seller will be treated with the utmost confidence

- We commit to finding the best win/win deal for all the parties concerned

- If we believe that selling your property to us is not the best solution for you, we will tell you and even help you with an alternative solution

- We commit to providing realistic timescales for the purchase of their property

- We guarantee that there are no hidden costs for the seller. The price we agree is the amount they will receive

- We will keep the seller informed and updated throughout the purchase process

- We will do what we say we will do and keep to our word

If you come from a place of trying to help the seller find a win/win solution, you will get more deals.

Chapter 5:

How to maximise cash flow from your property

One of the main benefits of investing in property is the significant capital gain you can make as your property rises in value over the long term. However, to benefit from the gain, you need to make sure you can afford to hold the property in the meantime. Ideally you don't want to have to support your property portfolio. Quite the opposite in fact! Your portfolio should support you financially. The rent you receive from your tenants should more than cover all the costs of ownership so that each month there is surplus cash profit left over for you to enjoy.

Investors who lose money are often the ones who get it wrong because of cash flow. They can't afford to hold their property and so have to sell which, depending on the market conditions, means they themselves may become motivated sellers. The purpose of this chapter is to help you ensure you maximise the cash flow from your investment properties.

So, let's go back to fundamentals for a moment. As a property investor, one of the essential skills you need to develop is the ability to assess a particular opportunity quickly to decide if it is a good investment and suitable for you or not.

What makes a good investment?

Now let's just remind ourselves of the first three of my Five Golden Rules of Investing:

1. Always buy from motivated sellers.

2. Buy in an area with strong rental demand.

3. Buy for cash flow.

Of course you want to pay as little as ethically possible for the property but the discount alone is not the only factor to consider. There is no point buying a property even with a great discount if you cannot rent it out easily and make a positive cash flow.

To help you focus on only buying good cash flow properties you could buy 'as if prices will never go up again', and so the only reason to buy would be for the great cash flow and return on investment.

When researching any potential investment there are two main factors we are concerned with. We want to determine:

A) The true market value of the property

B) The realistic market rent that could be achieved

This is the information that a mortgage company would want a chartered surveyor to collect on their behalf in order to assess whether to grant you an investment mortgage on a particular property. You need this information a long time before you even apply for the mortgage to decide if it is the right kind of investment for you.

With these two pieces of information you can ascertain whether you are going to make a profit each month after covering all of the expenses.

The main expense you will incur on a monthly basis is the interest on your investment mortgage. I have a very simple rule of thumb which you can use to assess this monthly expense.

For every £20,000 you borrow, at an interest rate of 6% you will pay £100 per calendar month (pcm) in interest. For example, if you were to borrow £80,000 it would cost you £400 pcm.

This is based on a 6% annual interest rate for two reasons: firstly, it's the average rate I had during my years of investing prior to the Global Financial Crisis; secondly, it keeps the numbers easy to calculate because every £20,000 you borrow costs just £100 pcm. I like to keep things as simple as possible.

If the average cost of a mortgage is only 4% per annum, then this rule of thumb is very conservative. This means that, in reality, £20,000 would not cost you as much as £100 pcm, but by using 6% in your calculations you are being very cautious, which is good because you don't want to be too optimistic.

When working out the cash flow, many investors are too optimistic on what the costs will be and they don't get it right.

It's better to be pessimistic and have a nice surprise by making more money than expected.

Does the investment stack up?

This is a top level assessment method you can use to quickly and easily calculate if a property will make cash flow or not. For this quick test we work out the monthly mortgage cost and then multiple this by 125% to work out the required rent. If the actual rent is more than this required rent, then the property will make cash flow.

For example, with a mortgage of £80k using my rule of thumb (for every £20k you borrow at 6% pa, it will cost you £100 pcm in interest) then monthly interest would be £400, so the required rent would be at least £500 (£400 x 125%).

In this example, if the monthly rent was £500, it may only just about cover the costs. However, if the monthly rent was £550, then it means you would probably make some cash flow from this property each month. If the rent was just £450, you wouldn't be making positive cash flow; in fact we know it's going to cost you around £50 each month.

In our quick and easy calculation, the extra 25% over and above the interest payments is an approximation of the other monthly costs. Some of the other monthly costs involved in property are:

Buy-to-Let insurance: This is specialist landlord insurance which covers not only the building and the contents, but also, if someone was to have an accident in your property and decided to sue you, your insurance would cover this as well. It is very important that you get the correct Buy-to-Let insurance in place and be aware that the cheapest will probably not give you all the cover you need.

Property management fees: You might have a letting agent looking after your property for you which will cost on average 10% of the rent each month. Many investors start by managing their own properties but I would suggest that, once you have a number of properties, you don't really want to do this. Using a letting agent will reduce your profit each month but you must value your own time. I doubt very much you want to just swap whatever your current job is and replace it with a job as a full-time property manager. I recommend you find a good letting agent to manage your property for you to make sure you don't have the hassle. Get a recommendation from other investors.

Service charge: If it's a leasehold property, you are going to have service charges which, calculated on a monthly basis, might be anywhere from £40 to £400 pcm depending on the facilities that are on offer at that particular development. The service charges pay for community facilities such as cleaning and electricity in the hallways and maintenance of the building. The building might have a concierge or lifts that need maintaining, which will increase the service charges. The costs can vary dramatically, so if you are buying a leasehold property it's really important to ask what the service charges are each month. There will also be a small ground rent charge, which might be a few hundred pounds a year.

Central heating insurance: If you have a gas supply in your property then it is a legal requirement to have a Gas Safety Certificate which needs to be renewed each year. This can be covered as part of your boiler insurance offered by British Gas and other suppliers. I have this insurance on all of my properties to make sure that if there's any problem with my central heating, I can get it fixed quickly at no cost to me. The other benefit is that the tenant calls the service supplier direct, they don't call me. That's great, because I don't get the hassle and they feel in control of resolving the issue. In my view, it's worth paying the insurance premium, which is about £15 to £20 per month depending on the property.

To summarise – you can work out quickly if a property stacks up, as follows:

1. Work out how much the mortgage is going to cost you.

2. Multiply the monthly interest by 125% to give the required rent.

3. Check that the actual rent is more than the required rent.

Having used this quick approximation, if the property does not stack up, you can move on to the next one without wasting too much time. If, however, it looks like it does stack up well, it may be worth spending a little more time to work out clearly the actual cash flow to help you decide if you want to purchase it.

It is worth noting here that when you take out an investment mortgage the lender will want to make sure that the property produces enough rental income to not only cover the cost of the monthly mortgage, but also the other costs, so that you do not need to subsidise it. For many years they have used the same calculation and multiplied the monthly interest by 125%. However, some lenders are more cautious and now want to make sure the property stacks up at 145% of the monthly interest payment. The calculation used by mortgage companies can change from time to time, and so it is best to get advice from your mortgage broker to find out the latest position.

How much cash flow can I expect for each property?

This really depends on the purchase price and the rent that can be achieved which varies dramatically around the country. Very often I hear investors complain that investments just don't stack up where they live.

Whilst I would agree that it is possible that investments may not stack up exactly where you live, I would suggest that there is almost certainly somewhere within 45 minutes' drive of where you live where the rents do stack up.

Where I live in the West Midlands, a mid-terrace property with three bedrooms and two reception rooms may be worth £160,000 and would attract a rental income of £850 per month. If you had a 75% mortgage on this property, the mortgage advance would be £120,000. My rule of thumb would suggest that this would cost £600 per month in interest payments. The rent multiplier would suggest that the monthly costs would be approximately £750 (£600 x 125%). With a monthly rental of £850 this would provide a positive cash flow of approximately £100 a month, which frankly, is not a lot to get excited about.

At this monthly profit, how many of these properties would you need to replace your monthly income? Probably more than you would care to own. With this kind of monthly profit, many people can't be bothered to invest in property, probably because they forget about the long-term benefits.

Yes, we need the property to cover its costs in the short term and make positive cash flow for us, but it is for the long-term benefits that we are investing. In 10 years' time this property could have doubled in value from £160,000 to maybe £320,000.

We understand the long-term benefits of property investing. How can we make the short-term look more attractive? Well, there are a number of ways we can increase the cash flow from our property investments.

How about letting to a Local Housing Authority tenant?

More and more landlords are deciding to let their properties to people claiming benefits because the rent that the Local Housing Authority (LHA) will pay for a property is often higher than the average market rent in the area.

The amount of rent that the LHA will pay depends on what the tenant is entitled to rather than the property itself. For example, a single mother with a few children of a certain age may be entitled to a three-bedroom house which will attract a higher LHA rate than a couple who want to rent the same house. A single mother may also make a great long-term tenant as she may want to stay in your investment property long term so that her children can settle in the local school.

Some investors don't like the idea of letting to LHA tenants as they feel their house may get trashed. Whilst there are some undesirable LHA tenants, I have found that the vast majority of people on benefits are decent people who just don't happen to or can't work. I have some fantastic tenants who are on benefits.

With any tenants, whether they are on benefits or not, you do need to carry out your tenant referencing to check them out. A word of warning here! You may do a credit check on someone and they have a good job and a great credit score, but something can happen in their life, such as being made redundant or the breakdown of a relationship, and suddenly they go off the rails and stop paying the rent. At least with an LHA tenant you know that they don't work and that the government is essentially paying their rent!

Only you can decide if you want to rent to LHA tenants in some of your properties. I suggest as a minimum you should contact your local council to find out what the LHA rates are in your area. Often you can buy ex-council properties for very good prices and put LHA tenants into these properties and make great cash flow. Generally ex-council properties have good-sized rooms and so can be easy to rent in the right locations.

Boost your rental income with multi-lets

Instead of a single Assured Short-hold Tenancy (AST) contract, one of the best ways to get cash flow from your property is to rent it out room by room on a multi-let basis. If you rent out individual rooms in a property to students or young professionals, the combined rent will be much higher than the rent achieved if you rent the property to a family.

In the previous example we considered a £160,000 property which we could rent to someone for £850 per month. Instead of renting this property to a family, you could rent out the rooms to a number of different people. Remember, the property had three bedrooms and two reception rooms, which could both be used as a bedroom, giving you four or five renting units. For this type of property, you would generally include in the rent the bills such as gas and electricity, community charge, etc. With a normal single AST rental contract, the tenants would be responsible for their own bills but in a shared house the rent is usually inclusive of utility bills and council tax. The rent you could charge each individual will vary based on the size of the room, facilities of the house and, of course, location of the property.

I have many of these multi-let properties, which accommodate four to five individuals, where I achieve an average rent of about £400 per room per month. This means that each month I receive a total income for the property of about £2,000. After taking out the cost of the bills, which is usually about £450 per month, I have over £1,550 in rental income, compared to £850 on a single AST contract. Take out the cost of the mortgage and I average between £500 to £1,000 positive cash flow every month from each of these houses, depending on the number of tenants. How many of these would you need to replace your income? You don't need to have 100 properties; just 6 would be more than enough for most people to be financially independent.

If you like the idea of renting out your properties on a multi- let basis to maximise your cash flow, there are a number of things you need to consider:

Property location: Location is always important when buying property, but particularly with a multi-let property. You need to make sure the property is in an area where your potential tenants would like to live. Things to consider will be public transport links, local facilities and amenities, proximity to their place of work.

The size of the rooms: In all of my rental properties I want to make sure that I can fit at least a queen-size bed, if not a double, into all of the bedrooms. For some reason, young professionals and students like to sleep in double beds. I don't know why! Then, where possible, we fit en-suite bathroom facilities into bedrooms making sure we still have enough room for wardrobes, chests of drawers and room to swing a cat! It is a good idea to check with your local council as they will have guidelines on minimum room sizes.

The number of rooms: As all of the utility bills are included in the rent, it is important to make sure you have at least four rentable rooms per property to spread the cost of the monthly bills. I have found that with only three tenants in the property, the extra amount that I need to charge each tenant makes the rent uncompetitive in my local market. The more tenants you have, the further you have to spread the cost of the bills. I believe six rentable rooms is the perfect number.

The quality of accommodation: Just because you are renting out your property on a room-by-room basis, don't think that you can provide sub-standard accommodation. Far from it; the quality of accommodation has to be high in order to attract your potential tenants. There is a lot of competition in the market, but I always maintain that if you have good quality accommodation in the right location at the right price, you should always be able to find suitable tenants. All of my multi-let properties are set up to a very high standard. Many of the bedrooms have private en-suite facilities; all of the properties are renovated to a high standard, coming with cable TV and broadband internet in every room.

HMO licensing

In July 2006, the government's legislation regarding Houses in Multiple Occupation (HMOs) was introduced, enforcing that any property with five or more tenants on three or more floors was legally obliged to be licensed by the local council. The interpretation of the law regarding licensing has been left to local authorities, so the criteria do vary from council to council. For example, in Swindon where I own a 4-bedroom property, on three floors, the Council has decided that any property on three or more floors with just three tenants needs to be licensed as an HMO. It is important to check with your local council to ensure that you keep up-to-date with all their housing regulations.

If you are operating an HMO property which requires mandatory licensing, you need to contact your local council to obtain a license application form. The process is actually quite simple, even if rather time-consuming. You complete the forms and submit them with your application fee, which I have seen vary from £1,000 to £3,000 (which is usually for five years). At some point your property will be inspected to make sure it meets all the relevant standards. Whether your multi-let property needs to be licensed or not, it still needs to adhere to the current safety standards regarding the fire doors, emergency exits and lights, etc. I recommend you contact your local council to seek guidance to ensure that you are providing suitable safe accommodation for your tenants.

Planning permission for multi-lets

Not to be confused with mandatory HMO licensing, this is a totally different matter. In April 2010 the then Labour government's housing minister introduced legislation designed to help local councils control the 'studentification' of certain areas. The Conservative Party had vowed to abolish this legislation if they came to power, which they did in May 2010 in a coalition with the Liberal Democrats. What actually happened was that the government decided to allow local councils to adopt Article 4 direction if they so wished, and many councils did.

Previously you could convert any normal house into an HMO, for up to six people under permitted development rights which means you did not need planning permission. Article 4 direction is where the permitted development rights have been withdrawn. What this means is that, in cases where Article 4 direction is in place, you need to apply for planning permission to turn a residential property into an HMO, if three or more unrelated people will be living there.

If, however, the property was already used as an HMO before Article 4 was introduced in your area (if at all), then that property automatically gets planning permission and you don't need to apply, as long as you can prove that is has continuously been rented out as a multi-let property.

One final point on planning permission is that if you have a large HMO with seven or more tenants, then you will definitely need to apply for planning permission to implement a change of use from a residential property to a commercial property.

The best thing to do is to check with the planning department at your local council.

Serviced Accommodation

Serviced Accommodation, or SA as it is known, is a strategy to maximise your rental income and works very well for one and two-bedroom apartments, in locations close to city centres and airports.

The concept is that you rent out a property on a very short-term basis, and so charge a premium rent for it. It is very similar to Furnished Holiday Lets. Usually you will provide cleaning and laundry services and the accommodation is furnished and looks very much like a hotel room.

Guests like to stay in SA for two main reasons:

1. If someone is staying away from home for more than a few nights, it can be quite impersonal and expensive staying in a hotel, where you only have one room and have to eat your meals in the hotel restaurant. Whereas if you rent the whole apartment, you have a lot more space, can enjoy the living room and use the kitchen.

2. It can also be more cost effective for a group of people staying together. For example, a one-bedroom apartment could sleep four people. Two in the bedroom and two on a bed settee in the living room. This would probably be cheaper than renting two hotel rooms. A two-bed apartment could sleep six people.

The main benefit for you is that you could earn a much higher income than if you rented the property out to a standard tenant on a six-month contract.

A one-bed apartment that might normally rent out for say £750 per month might get anywhere between £50 and £100 per night. Of course the property is unlikely to be full all the time. 70% occupancy is a good rate to aim for. The rent you can achieve will very much depend on the size of the property, the location and the completion in the area.

Of course there are higher costs involved. First of all, you would take on the cost of running the property such as council tax, broadband internet, TV licence, water rates, gas and electricity costs. In addition to this, you would need to pay for cleaning the property in between guest stays, and cover the costs of changing and laundering bed sheets and towels which you would provide. You would need to employ a part-time housekeeper to do the change-overs for you unless you want to do it yourself, which is not a good idea as it can be time and labour intensive.

There are all sorts of people who want to stay in this type of accommodation varying from contractors working away from home, people on weekend city breaks, tourists, and people visiting family and friends. You can find them by advertising your property on websites such as Airbnb and booking.com. These sites will charge you each time they find guests for you.

A couple of things you need to look out for. Always make sure you take payment in advance before the guests arrive. Make sure you have appropriate insurance in place, and also check, if you have a leasehold property, that your freeholder is happy with the property being used in this way.

If you have single-let properties which don't make enough cash flow, then if they are in the right location it might be possible to turn them into serviced accommodation and thus into profitable units. Another benefit of this strategy is that the rental income is not affected by Section 24 tax changes because these are treated like Furnished Holiday Lets.

If you don't have any properties suitable to be used as Serviced Accommodation, then maybe you could find other landlords who use the Rent to Rent strategy.

Rent to Rent strategy

A great strategy that we have been teaching on the Property Mastermind Programme since 2007 is called Rent to Rent. This is where, you find a motivated landlord who is happy to rent their property to you for a guaranteed rental income on a three to five years contract. You then re-purpose the property and rent it out in a different way such as HMO or SA.

You then make the margin between what you pay the landlord and the rent you receive from the tenants, less the bills. This can make almost as much profit as you would earn if you owned the property without having to get a mortgage or put down a big deposit.

This is not to be confused with sub-letting, which is not allowed by most mortgage companies. It is important to get the correct contracts in place to make sure that everything is done properly. You can either take the property on effectively as a managing agent, and so issue AST contracts on behalf of the landlord as their agent, or you can get a commercial lease under which you can issue AST contracts.

The landlord is fully aware of what you are doing and happy to do this because you offer them a guaranteed rent with no voids. This works particularly well with retiring or tired landlords who don't want the hassle of managing the property themselves any more.

This is a popular strategy with new investors as it can be one of the quickest ways to generate cash flow without a huge investment. It is also a great way to see if you like HMOs or SA before making a large investment.

I can't teach you everything you need to know about Rent to Rent in these pages but I want to make sure you are aware of the strategy. I have made a video to explain more of this strategy which is available for you on the free pin App, details of which are in Chapter 8.

Case Study:
David Lockett

I am originally from Walsall and when I started the Property Mastermind Programme I was a 51-year-old accountant running my own small practice with three employees. I was doing ok in my business but I noticed that many of my successful clients had either made their money in property or invested their business profits into property, and so I wanted to learn how I could also invest in property to generate sufficient additional income, to allow me to work part time.

However, just three months into my Property Mastermind Programme something happened that motivated me to build a property business to completely replace my income so that I could spend more time with my wife and family. This incident was the tragic death of a good friend of mine who was younger than me. This changed my life and helped me realise what was important to me.

I knew I wanted to develop a property portfolio using Serviced Accommodation to generate a high income, and since I didn't have a lot of spare money I decided to focus on the rent to rent strategy. My first deal was sourced through a local letting agent who attends the Cheltenham property investors network (pin) meeting every month and really understands landlords. I discussed the type of property I wanted, a one or two-bed flat close to Cheltenham town centre, and what I would be using it for. Within a few days I had three viewings lined up. The third one of these was perfect, a two-bed apartment in a block of four within easy walking distance from the town centre and the local hospital. We agreed the corporate lease, which had to be altered to allow us to sub-let the apartment to our guests, and then we set about furnishing it and advertising it on booking.com and airbnb, etc. This was a massive learning experience, but once we had done it once we knew we could simply repeat the process a number of times and develop our business.

A summary of the deal is as follows:

- Property sourced through a local letting agent at a pin meeting
- Upfront furnishing costs around £2,400
- Monthly rental to the landlord of £750
- Council and other bills of approx. £250
- Average booking fees of £160
- Monthly income varied but typically £1,700
- Total monthly profit of £567, which is an ROI of 283%

Over the course of our Property Mastermind journey I took on a number of properties like this which meant that I was able to sell my accountancy practice and move into property full time. Since then I have set up a business working with another investor I met though Mastermind, which helps others achieve a sound income from Serviced Accommodation. More importantly, my wife Beverley, who is a teacher, has been able to go part time and we are now looking forward to spending more time together.

Home owner multi-let strategy

I am often asked by first-time buyers how they can get on to the property ladder. My standard answer is usually that they should buy a property with a number of rooms, so they can rent out the spare rooms to their friends or other young professionals. This is how I purchased my very first property. I had graduated from the University of Birmingham in debt and I was unemployed. Eventually, I secured a very good job at Cadbury Ltd in Birmingham and I decided that, rather than renting, I would love to buy my first property. As it was my own home I was able to obtain a 95% mortgage. I didn't have any deposit at all, so I needed to borrow the remaining 5% from a family member, for which I paid them interest. Although I didn't know it at the time, my first property purchase was in fact a No Money Down Deal as the entire purchase was funded with other people's money. I then rented out the two spare rooms in my home to two of my friends who were still studying at university. This worked really well for me as their rent covered the cost of the mortgage, and I was just left to pay the household bills, which I would have had to pay anyway. So really, I was living almost rent-free.

I believe this is probably the best strategy that any young person can use to get on the property ladder. Property is now far more expensive than when I purchased my first home. However, it is easier to get finance now than it was when I first started to invest. A first-time buyer can now obtain a mortgage, whereby a parent can be used as a guarantor or even the parent's income can be taken into account with some lenders. It is always best to check with your independent mortgage broker to find out what is possible right now.

The most important thing is to make sure the first-time buyer can afford the mortgage. If they are renting out a few of the rooms in their property, they should be able to cover the cost of the mortgage. This then leaves the question of how they raise a deposit to purchase the property. My solution would be to borrow the deposit from someone, such as a family member or friend, who already owns a property. The property owner may have plenty of equity in their property. The first-time buyer could approach the family member and suggest an opportunity for them to get involved in the property investment by lending that first-time buyer the deposit to buy the property.

Taking this strategy one step further, it's a great way for a young person to buy a property while they're still a student at university. Many parents purchase properties for their kids while they are studying at university, but they do it in the wrong way. Here is a great strategy to take advantage of tax savings.

Student multi-let strategy

Accommodation for students at university can be very expensive. Many parents with children at university have realised that paying for university accommodation for three or four years is dead money. For this reason, many parents decide to purchase a student property to accommodate their children and their friends whilst they are at university. Instead of being a drain on resources, this can actually make money, as property in the right student locations always seems to go up in value due to the high turnover and continual demand.

Most parents will release equity from their own home to raise a deposit for the investment property, which they purchase with a BTL mortgage in their own name. Their children and their friends then become the tenants. Although this is a good strategy, it fails to take advantage of several tax benefits that would be achieved if the property is purchased in the student's name instead of the parents' names.

The parents would release equity from their own home in exactly the same way to raise a deposit, but rather than purchasing a BTL property in their name, they would help their child purchase a residential property using a first-time buyer mortgage. This scenario, where the student is the owner of the property, has several tax advantages:

1. The student will be able to receive rental income from the property and use their personal tax allowances to mitigate any Income Tax liability. They will be able to earn £7,500 on the Rent a Room scheme and, in addition to this, a further £11,850 using their personal tax allowance (based on 2018-2019 tax allowances). This means they could earn over £19,000 in rental

income and pay no tax on this revenue. If the property was in the parents' name, any profits would be taxed at the parents' marginal income tax rate.

2. Once the student has finished university, they may decide either to hold on to the property or to sell. Any revenue generated from the sale of the property will be totally tax-free as this will have been the primary residence for the student. If the property was in the parents' name, any profits would be subject to Capital Gains Tax.

If the student decides to hold on to the property, as the value increases they could re-mortgage it to release the original deposit which can be returned to the parents. This is a far more tax-efficient way of doing it, which also helps the student build their credit rating.

The buy to sell strategy

When I buy property I like to hold it for the long term. I don't like to sell it just to make some short-term cash. However, when you are sourcing below market value properties, you will come across some properties that may not be suitable to rent out. Probably the market rents in the area are insufficient to support the BTL mortgage and the location may not be suitable to let the property out on a multi-let basis.

Rather than walking away from the deal, it may be possible to buy the property at the discounted rate and sell it on at a higher price for a cash profit.

This can be a fantastic strategy for making you some extra cash. Remember that if you sell any property other than your primary residence, you have to pay Capital Gains Tax on the profit if the property has been rented out. If, however, you buy it and sell it on without renting it to any tenants, then this is considered trading property and you would pay Income Tax on the profit instead of Capital Gains Tax. It is well worth speaking to a property accountant before you start selling property to make sure you minimise your tax liability.

Many investors actually plan to sell at least one of their rental properties each year to take advantage of their annual capital gains allowance. Personally, I want to make sure that in any given year I always buy more properties than I sell, so that the net effect is that my portfolio is always growing in size.

The other consideration, of course, is the ease with which you will be able to sell the property. I believe it is always a risky strategy when the market is static or in decline. You may have to hold on to the property for a long time or discount the price substantially in order to sell it. You need to consider the market conditions at the time to see if this is an appropriate strategy.

I wanted to share this strategy with you so that you know what to do when we have the right market conditions. I am currently finding below market value properties and then selling them on to first-time buyers and amateur investors who do not expect discounts as large as I would want. If you are buying and 'flipping', there are some tips you need to follow:

Make sure you get a big enough discount

To buy and flip a property, my rule of thumb is that you need to purchase it for at least 25% below the true market value. This is because to make any money you need to get a large enough discount to cover the purchase costs, sale costs and holding costs, and allow for the property to be sold on to the end consumer at a small discount. I recommend you sell it at slightly less than the market value, to ensure that the price is competitive compared to similar properties on the market at the same time. For example, if you were able to buy a property worth £160,000 for just £120,000, you would maybe put it on the market with an estate agent at £139,950 to sell it quickly.

Make sure you can cover the holding costs

The property may take a while to sell on the open market. Until it is sold you will have to cover all of the holding costs such as the interest payments on the mortgage, insurance, and maybe council tax, etc. The longer it takes to sell the property, the higher your holding costs will be, so you need to make sure you have enough cash flow to cover these costs.

Use a great estate agent

The time taken to sell your property depends partly on the quality of the estate agent you use. Selecting the right estate agent is vital, and you want one who is proactive and has lists of investors and buyers looking for the type of property that you have to sell. They should be able to advise you on the price at which you need to put the property on the market to achieve a quick sale. Make sure that you keep on top of them to find out what they're doing to sell the property for you. I usually work with estate agents with whom I already have a relationship as I know they will work harder for me to sell the property. Don't try to beat them down on their selling commission, as they need to be motivated to sell the property for you. You may even want to offer them bonus commission for selling quickly.

Make the property appealing

When you buy a property below market value it can often look old and tired. To attract a buyer who is prepared to purchase the property at a good price, you need to make sure that the property looks desirable. Spending some money on cosmetic improvements should prove to be a worthwhile investment of your money. We have all seen the home improvement programmes on television which show you how to prepare a house for sale. It is amazing what a difference a tidy-up and a fresh coat of paint can have on a property. You need to budget for any improvements and make sure you spend your money wisely. Places where you can add value to a property include the kitchen and bathroom. The general appearance of the property should be clean and tidy. Make sure any rubbish and debris is removed from the back yard and the front garden and ensure you maintain the gardens while the property is on the market. It is worth spending a few hundred pounds to dress the property with some colour, pictures and mirrors, and make sure it always smells nice with the use of plug-in air fresheners.

CASE STUDY:
Dave Guest

Up until the age of 32, my background was in IT, and although I've always enjoyed this work it never really gave me the lifestyle I wanted, and I realised I needed to find a way to boost my income.

After lots of research, looking at different income streams, I discovered, to my surprise, that property investing really interested me.

I ultimately enrolled in the Mastermind Programme and pretty quickly decided my strategy was going to be flipping properties. I seemed to have a knack for finding run-down places that I would then refurbish and sell on at a profit on the open market, usually making around £13k-£15k per deal.

As enjoyable as it is for me to transform a property and sell it on, it does not come without its stresses, i.e. managing trades, unforeseen issues, etc. And, of course, the time involved to release the profit out of the deal. This whole cycle can often take 8 to 12 months for many reasons, with the biggest delay often being the time it takes to sell.

However, whilst on Mastermind, I learned all about a strategy that dramatically reduced the time it took to run through this cycle: it was selling run-down properties at auction. Let me give you an example of one of my deals.

I found a property on the internet which was a 3-bed detached house in Walsall, West Midlands, that was originally marketed for offers over £165k. This was far too expensive, considering its condition, but it caught my attention because I knew at this price other buyers would be put off, and realised that there were probably very few offers made for the property, and so the sellers might be motivated.

Not only did it need around £25k of decorative work, there also appeared to be a structural issue, as there were some cracks, suggesting one corner of the house might be subsiding. It would not be possible to get a mortgage on this property and so it would have to be purchased for cash, which further reduced the number of potential buyers.

I knew that with underpinning to resolve the structural issue and full refurbishment, this property would conservatively achieve £175k, and so I used this figure as a starting point with the agent and we worked back from there. I used the potential structural issue as leverage to bring down my offer.

Although the property had been on the market for some considerable time, the vendors initially rejected my low offer, and so I put the property in my follow-up system as I was taught to do whilst on the Property Mastermind Programme. Nineteen months later I purchased the property for just £80k.

I wasn't as concerned about the structural issue or condition of the property as many other buyers might have been, because I knew that if I put it into the auction at a low enough price, the auction would forgive this property its faults and an auction buyer would just be focused on the perception of buying a house at a BIG "discount".

I listed the property in July with a local auction house, with a guide price of £75k - £80k, with no reserve and the fees to be covered by the buyer. Needless to say at this low price there was a lot of interest, and on the day the property sold for £96k, giving me a profit of £16k, which was paid to me 10 days later.

In the two months that I had owned this property, I had only visited it twice, and did no work on it whatsoever. All that was required was to understand the market I was selling to.

Summary of the deal as follows:

- I found this property openly available on the internet
- Property was originally listed for offers over £165k but I eventually paid £80k after 19 months of follow up
- I put it straight into an auction without doing any work to it
- Sold the property for £96k with the buyer picking up my costs
- £16k profit which is a 20% return on my investment in just two months

To do this strategy successfully, you need to know your area well and have a good understanding of what properties will sell for, and what work needs to be done to a property to ensure that the person you sell to can still make a profit. This will ensure that you have lots of potential buyers at the auction interested in purchasing your property.

Cash for selling leads and deals

When you start to generate your own motivated seller leads you will no doubt come across a number of deals which represent great investment opportunities but which don't fit your personal investment strategy. It is possible for you to make a very good income from selling leads that you don't want to other investors.

A number of the properties that I have purchased from motivated sellers have come from another investor who specialises in sourcing leads. This investor spends a huge amount of money advertising to attract motivated sellers. Out of the hundreds of people who call him every single month, he will discount many, because they are not true motivated sellers. However, from all the calls he receives, he will usually find at least a few sellers where there is, potentially, a good deal. Now, of course, the investor will take some of the best deals for himself as one might expect, but often he will get a deal that is outside his geographic area which he has no interest in purchasing. These are some of the deals that he passes on to me and a few other selected investors with whom he is working. I pay this investor 2% of the purchase price (plus VAT) for every deal that actually goes through. I have a good relationship with him, whereby I only pay if the deal actually happens.

There is a great opportunity for you to make money in exactly the same way. The amount of money which you can generate will depend very much on the quality of the lead and how qualified it is. For example, if you pass on the name and address and property details of a motivated seller that you have not contacted, which means the lead may be unqualified, you may be able to sell this kind of lead on a website for somewhere between £50 and £150. However, the way to make money is to find qualified leads that you can pass on to other investors. A qualified lead is one where you will have spoken to the seller, assessed the situation, provided a certain amount of background research, and maybe even agreed a price in principle with the seller. In short, you have done a lot of the legwork for another investor to whom you sell the deal.

Taking this one stage further, on a Fully Packaged Done Deal you could charge anywhere between 1% and 4% of the purchase price, depending on the nature of the deal. This could generate thousands of pounds for every deal package you supply to other investors. At this level of income, how many deals would you need to package for other investors each month to replace your current monthly income?

The very best way for you to make money selling these types of qualified leads and packaged deals is to develop your own network of investors who you can pass qualified leads on to. You'd need to make sure your investors know what they are doing and how to convert the leads into a completed property purchase so that you get paid. There is absolutely no point in you wasting a fantastic lead on an amateur investor who won't know what to do with it and may blow the deal because of their inexperience.

As part of my Property Mastermind Programme, we have an online forum where the Mastermind members can promote their unwanted deals to one another. Because everyone on the Mastermind Programme knows what they're doing, there is only a small chance that the deal will fall over through lack of experience. There is also a high level of trust in the group that everyone will act ethically in their dealings with each other and the motivated sellers.

CASE STUDY:
Andrew Tonks

I have recently left the military, where I was a helicopter pilot for 10 years, to become an airline pilot. My reason for investing in property is to provide security for my family should I no longer be able to fly due to medical reasons and to have more freedom and choice in how we live our lives.

One of my original strategies was Rent to Rent and through my direct marketing to landlords, I found one who said that he was interested in using my service. I met him at the property and after looking around sat down to talk to him and try to understand his circumstances. He then said that he'd been renting to students but was tired of managing it himself and having to decorate and tidy up the property every year, whilst also sometimes struggling to get them to stay a full year.

The property was a modern two-bedroom flat in a good area of Central London and I explained that I could offer him a guaranteed rental service and only use corporate/professional tenants on a contract let basis which he liked the sound of. I discovered that the landlord owned some other properties in the same block and would be happy to do a similar deal if this worked well.

I did my due diligence on the property and worked out that it would cost around £1,000 to get the property in a good enough condition to attract professional short-term tenants. I could afford to pay the landlord a rental figure of between £1,800-£2,100pcm. After some negotiation we agreed on a deposit of £2,000 and a monthly rent of £2,000, which would bring in £525 profit each month after all expenses based on 70% occupancy levels.

A few weeks later my strategy changed and I realised that although the deal was good, it no longer fitted my strategy and that I might not have the time to give it my full attention. I was about to call the landlord and say that the deal was off but then remembered Simon Zutshi and my Mastermind coach saying that if a deal doesn't work for you, it may do for somebody else. I initially started to panic a little as this was way outside my comfort zone having only been on the Property Mastermind for a couple of months. I had not dealt with this situation before and felt unsure of the best way ahead. However, I then remembered that another member of my Mastermind Programme was a deal packager and might be able to assist. I called him up and after a very helpful conversation knew what I had to do to package the deal for another investor. Using the Mastermind online forum, I got the required documents and then I spoke to the landlord and explained that my circumstances had changed but that I worked with a large pool of investors, and if he was happy, I could find somebody else to take on the property. As the landlord and I had built up a good rapport during our previous meetings, he said that he was more than happy for me to help him find another investor to take on his property.

After advertising the deal online, I quickly got an investor who wanted to view the property. I spoke to him a few times and did my due diligence on him before arranging a viewing. This went well and after sorting out the paperwork we agreed a fee of £3,000 with a £500 deposit to secure the deal. The investor got the keys a few weeks later and the landlord was very happy with the end result and said that he'd be happy for me to take on his other properties or help him find other investors who would.

A summary of the deal:

- Property sourced through direct marketing
- Monthly rent to landlord £2,000 plus a £2,000 deposit
- Profit per month after costs based on 70% occupancy £525
- Sourcing fee £3,000
- Total amount of time put into deal – 14 hours

Since joining the Mastermind Programme my level of property knowledge has increased 10-fold. I'm in the process of taking on several HMOs on a rent to rent and purchase basis. I am also hoping to purchase a block of flats with a view to splitting the title and releasing all the initial funds put in. The course has opened my eyes to how to be more successful and professional in property investing and the

> power of your network. All going well I should have replaced the income from my military pilot job before the year long course is finished. This gives my family freedom to do what we want and security should our circumstances ever change.

Please note, if you are selling deals or properties you should register with the estate agents' ombudsman to make sure you comply with all of the regulations. You should also have professional indemnity insurance and make sure you understand and adhere to the anti-money laundering regulations.

Summary of strategies to make cash flow:

1. Could you make more money letting to LHA tenants?

2. Can you multi-let your property?

3. Could you use the property as Serviced Accommodation?

4. Could you use Rent to Rent?

5. Buy to sell in the right market conditions.

6. Selling deals to other investors.

Chapter 6:

A new strategy for property investors

Purchase Options have been used for many years in the area of commercial property and development, for example, in relation to land purchases. However the use of Purchase Lease Options in residential property investing is relatively new here in the UK, despite being established in the USA and Australia.

There is a great deal of ignorance and misunderstanding surrounding the topic of Purchase Options and whether or not they are legal. Please don't expect to learn everything you need to know about Options in just one chapter. In fact, I have written a new book all about this one strategy because I believe Options are such a useful tool for property investors. However, the purpose of this chapter is to give you an awareness of Purchase Options and an understanding of what they are and, more importantly, how you can use them for the mutual benefit of both yourself and the motivated seller.

What are Purchase Options and Purchase Lease Options?

A Purchase Option is a legal agreement which gives you the control of an asset without actually owning it.

To keep it simple, I'm going to break it down into its various elements:

- An Option is the right to buy, but not the obligation to do so, at a fixed price, within a certain time period.

Taking this one step further, a Purchase Lease Option (PLO) is the same as a Purchase Option, with the additional benefit of:

- Being able to use the assets in return for a monthly lease (rental) payment.

What this means is that you can control a property and gain a rental income from it, without the need for the usual 25% deposit or even a mortgage!

This can be extremely attractive to anyone who wants to invest in property, but for whatever reason is unable to obtain a mortgage and / or does not have a large deposit.

It sounds too good to be true!

Very often when investors first hear about Options, they are sceptical because the concept sounds too good to be true. Why on earth would the seller agree to grant you an option on their property?

Remember the underlying essence of this book is all about you finding motivated sellers who have a property related problem and then creating an ethical win/win solution. In certain circumstances, a PLO could be the ideal solution for the seller.

The easiest way to explain this is with an example:

Peter is the owner of a property, which in today's market is worth about £200k, and he has a mortgage on the property of £195k. In this situation, there would be absolutely no point in you making Peter a below market value offer for his property, because he needs the full asking price to be able to clear the outstanding mortgage.

Even if Peter found a buyer who was prepared to purchase the property at the full market value, by the time he has paid estate agency and legal fees, it is unlikely that he will make any money from the sale of the property. This raises an interesting question. If Peter is not going to get any money from the sale, why is he selling?

It's really important to understand this point. Sometimes the vendor may be selling a property, not because they want to raise money from the sale, but simply because they do not want the property, or the mortgage debt associated with it.

Maybe the monthly payments on the mortgage are a financial burden to Peter that he would rather not have. Although the sale of the property would not raise any income, it would mean that he would no longer need to find the money to pay the mortgage each month. This could be a logical reason for Peter wanting to get rid of the property.

In this situation, maybe we can help Peter as follows. We tell Peter that we would be prepared to purchase the property at full market value (or maybe slightly more) in a few years time, and in the meantime we make all of the monthly mortgage payments for him. In a way, we are babysitting Peter's mortgage for him. This could be a great solution for Peter, but what could possibly be in it for us?

Let's say that Peter's mortgage payments are £600 per month and this property would rent out for £1,000 a month. As long as the property is in an area with strong rental demand, then you could potentially benefit from a couple of hundred pounds from a property that you don't own.

Now you may be thinking, "If the cash flow on this property is so good, why doesn't the owner just let out the property themselves?"

One possible answer to this very valid question is that usually the owner doesn't want the hassle or risk of being a landlord. Maybe they're worried about bad tenants or void periods when they would need to cover the costs themselves. Maybe they have been a landlord previously and experienced some of these problems, and now they are just fed up and want to get rid of the problem.

The main benefit to the owner for granting you a PLO is that you commit to pay their mortgage every month, whether or not the property is tenanted. This peace of mind and certainty may be more important to the owner than making a few hundred pounds per month.

How do you like the idea of benefiting from the cash flow and potential equity growth without the need to get a mortgage in your own name?

Case Study: Dave Morris

In my corporate life I was a sales director in the IT industry based in Solihull in the West Midlands but now I am a full-time property investor having become financially independent whilst on the Property Mastermind Programme.

One of the first deals I did was a three-storey, seven-bedroom licensed HMO in the centre of Birmingham. It was in an auction catalogue with a guide price of £180k. I had viewed it directly with the vendor and established his motivation; the property was a 90-minute drive from his home, so any maintenance issues, inspections or viewings were a challenge, and he and his family were about to emigrate to Australia! It is important to note at this stage that I was a novice investor in the eyes of the banks, so even if they would lend to me, the best LTV I could get was 60% so I needed a £72k deposit and some hefty fees.

I made the owner an offer which was rejected because it was well below the guide price, and the house went to auction for the first time but failed to sell, so it was a case of following up and seeing what would work for the vendor. I thought that a Purchase Lease Option might work, so we sat down and discussed what was important to him and it became clear that the vendor needed two things: firstly, to be able to walk away from the property to follow his wife, who had now gone to Australia; and secondly, to release the equity to fund the purchase of their new home when he got there.

In an ideal scenario, for a Purchase Lease Option, the vendor wouldn't need the money now; however the equity was only a fraction of the cost of the deposit so I felt it could still work.

We agreed the Heads of Terms for the Purchase Lease Option but the vendor was still keen to try the auction one more time, so I sat in the front row waiting to see what happened. It had a fixed reserve of £182k and bidding stopped at £180k so the Option was now on, and it was a case of using specialist solicitors to draw up the legal contracts for both myself and the vendor.

Summary of the deal as follows:

- I approached the seller after the property failed to sell in a local auction
- Agreed purchase price of £178k any time in the next seven years, less the £30k upfront Option fee
- Costs were: monthly lease fee of £100, monthly mortgage of £184, and bills including letting fee of £640
- Rental income of £2,020 with a monthly profit of £1,096
- Return on investment is 44%

As I built on my education with Simon it became clear that with a deal that was this good I could secure investment from someone else and therefore reduce my personal investment.

How to spot a potential PLO

There are two specific criteria to look at which will help you identify potential PLO deals.

The first and most important criterion is that the vendor doesn't need money from the sale of the property. Most people selling a property are doing so because they do actually require the money for something. If that's the case, then a PLO would probably not be suitable for them because with the Option they are not going to receive the money they need now.

If, however, they are selling the property because they don't want it, and they don't need the cash from the sale (or as in the example above with Peter, there may be no cash left after clearing the mortgage), then a PLO could be a viable solution.

PLOs work really well when there are properties for sale on the open market that have no equity, or are in negative equity, whereby the mortgage debt is higher than the value of the property.

The second criterion to look at is what I call "Favourable Mortgage Conditions". To meet these conditions, the owner's mortgage should ideally be:

On a relatively low interest rate

Due to the record low Bank of England base rate, many people are fortunate to be paying very low interest rates on their mortgages. These rates are often lower than the interest rate you would pay when taking out a new mortgage; which means that, by "babysitting" the owner's mortgage, the monthly payments may be less than the payments you would make on your mortgage if you purchased the property. Essentially, this means there is more cash flow profit for you every month.

An interest only mortgage

If the owner's mortgage is interest only, then the monthly payments will be less than in the case of a repayment mortgage. It's not necessarily a deal breaker if the seller has a repayment mortgage, but you will make less monthly cash flow.

A Buy-to-Let mortgage

If the owner has a residential mortgage, and you intend to rent out the property, then you should ideally seek approval from the owner's mortgage company, referred to as 'Consent to Let'. If the seller is a landlord, then they will probably have a BTL mortgage in which case it automatically includes Consent to Let, which makes the process far easier for all concerned.

No mortgage at all

Sometimes investors incorrectly think that this strategy only works if there is no equity in the property. It might be the case that the property is unencumbered, in other words there is no mortgage at all. This can also work very well for a PLO because we can give the owner a better return on their money than if they were to sell their property and put the money in the bank. If there is no mortgage, then a PLO can work really well, as long as the owner does not need the money from the sale now.

If both of these criteria are in place, then there is a good chance that a PLO could work well. Given the choice, most vendors would prefer a clean sale rather than a PLO, so you need to be able to explain simply how an Option could benefit both you and them.

The easiest way to find PLOs

By now you are probably thinking, "This sounds great – how do I find vendors who would be happy to grant me a PLO on their property?"

Instead of just looking for PLOs which won't be a viable solution for many vendors – particularly those selling because they urgently need the cash now – a more successful strategy would be to focus on finding motivated sellers (as described earlier in this book), for whom PLOs could be an appropriate solution.

Having said this, I want to highlight two particular types of motivated sellers for whom PLOs could work really well.

The first type is the vendor who has a property listed with an estate agent and a letting agent at the same time (I am sure you will have noticed this in the past). This would suggest that the vendor probably wants to sell, but is struggling to do so and thus is prepared to rent until they can sell. This is exactly what you are proposing with a PLO. You will pay them a monthly rent until you buy it at some point in the future.

The second type of vendor is the tired or retiring landlord, who no longer wants the hassle of their BTL property. I find this type of vendor may also be more open to creative solutions than the average motivated seller. You can find these landlords by looking in newspapers, or online for those landlords who are renting their properties, or you may even meet them at property networking events.

What to say to property owners?

When speaking to a vendor, never use the words "Purchase Lease Option", or PLO, as most people will have no idea what you're talking about. You need to keep the language really simple, make sure you understand their problem and then demonstrate how you can solve their problem.

There are two simple questions you can ask the property owner to determine if they would consider granting you a PLO on their property.

1. Would you be interesting in renting your property on a long-term let for between three to five years?

2. Would you be interested in selling the property to me at some point in the future?

If they answer yes to both of these questions, then there is a good chance that a PLO could work. It then comes down to a matter of negotiation around the purchase price, the length of the option and the monthly payment.

What about legal contracts?

To make the PLO agreement legally binding you need to pay a financial consideration to the seller in return for the Option to buy. This option fee is usually just £1, but depending on the nature and size of the deal could be several thousand pounds.

One of the main benefits for you doing a PLO is that you have the right to buy, but not the obligation to do so. The vendor, on the other hand, is contractually obliged to sell to you if you want to exercise your Option to buy.

This could cause some potential problems. Imagine that you help a motivated seller who is now desperate to get rid of their property which has no equity, and so you take on the responsibility to pay their mortgage and have the right to buy in five years at the current market value of £200k. In five years' time that property could increase in value to say £270k. Five years can be a long time and the vendor may decide that they don't really want to sell you the property worth £270k for just £200k.

Whilst PLO contracts are legally binding, and at the time the vendor was all too happy to sign, I predict that in the very near future there could be "no win, no fee" solicitors delighted to help vendors get out of these agreements because they may seem "unfair", or they may even claim that the vendor didn't know what they were agreeing to.

For this reason, it is very important that both you and the vendor obtain independent legal advice to ensure that everyone understands exactly what they are committing to.

The challenge here is that because PLOs are quite new, most solicitors don't understand what they are and so could even put their clients off considering them. For this reason, we always use two firms of solicitors from our power team who understand Options and work well together. One firm represents you and the other one represents the vendor to ensure that they understand the implications.

All you need to do is to agree the 'Heads of Terms' with the vendor and then forward these to your solicitor who will draw up the legal contracts for you.

The 'Heads of Terms' need to include:

1. Your full name and home address

2. The vendor's full name and home address

3. The address of the property in question

4. The agreed option fee (at least £1)

5. The amount for which you can purchase the property

6. The length of the Option period

7. Any monthly lease (if applicable)

8. Any special terms and conditions

What else can you do with Options?

There is so much you can do with Options. In this chapter I have just scratched the surface, but I wanted to make you aware of how these powerful tools could help you and some of the motivated sellers that you will find.

I love the flexibility of options and the creativity with which they can be used to help solve people's problems. For this reason I have written a book called *No Mortgage Required* all about PLOs and how you can profit from using them.

For the time being, let me just share a few ideas on how you could use PLOs:

Upgrade your own living accommodation

When you take out a PLO on a property, you don't have to rent it out to a tenant. You could decide to live there yourself. One of my Mastermind delegates did this on a large empty property in the village where he lives. He has moved into this large house, which is almost twice the size of his own home which he has managed to rent out for about the same amount as he pays in monthly Options fees. The net effect is that he now lives in a house twice the size of his own home, at no extra cost.

If you are currently renting, this could also be a great way for you to get your foot onto the property ladder.

Flip property using Options

Many investors like the idea of buying property at a discount, adding some value and then selling it on at a higher price. Rather than having to put in a deposit and get a mortgage to buy the property, why not just control it with an Option and flip it through an auction or add value and then sell it on?

Control an overseas holiday home

You can also use PLOs on holiday homes. There are plenty of overseas property owners who do not want their properties any more, but are unable to sell them.

The owners may be happy to receive a low rental all year round with no hassle, which could allow you to make a huge profit renting the property out week by week in peak season.

If you are going to do this, you need to do your research, just as you would with any investment, to make sure there is sufficient rental demand in the area, at the correct rental rate, to make it worth your while.

Multi-let – high cash flow strategy

This is a strategy that we have taught on the Property Mastermind Programme for many years and it is probably one of the most popular, with the increasing popularity of HMO properties, as described in the last chapter.

The idea is that you find a large property which the landlord is struggling to rent out on a single-let basis. You offer to pay the landlord a guaranteed rent for three to five years on a commercial lease. As long as the property is in the right location, it may be possible to rent out the individual rooms, which will achieve a rent far higher than the single-let rent. This means you can make between £500 to £2,000 profit on a property that you don't own or even have a mortgage on.

This is very similar to the Rent to Rent strategy described in Chapter 5, with the added benefit that you have the right to buy the property anytime during the option period for the agreed option price. This means that you could benefit from the capital growth as well as the high cash flow during the option period.

If you would like to learn more about PLOs then you can check out my second book which is available on this website:

www.NoMortgageRequiredBook.co.uk

Chapter 7:

You don't have to do everything on your own

You need your own Power Team

One of the secrets of being a successful property investor is having a team of people around you who can help you achieve your goals. This group of individuals and companies will help you to achieve far more than you could possibly do on your own. Setting up a good Power Team is one of the first things you should do before even looking for investment opportunities. It's no good finding an amazing deal and then missing out on it, just because you can't move quickly enough.

With the correct Power Team in place, whenever you find a deal, you just pass the details on to your team and they will get on with it for you. Your role will then be to chase everyone to ensure the deal happens satisfactorily. You need to ensure that the different elements of your power team can work together effectively. They need to understand exactly what you're doing and the way you do it.

It is really important that the members of your team are very good at what they do. They should be doing their particular element every day. If you find that you have to explain to someone in your team what you require and they don't get it quickly enough, then they may not have the required knowledge and so not be right for you. Don't waste your time trying to educate your team. Instead find someone else who is already doing what you want them to do.

The best way to set up your own Power Team is to get word-of-mouth recommendations from other successful investors who you can meet at pin meetings and property training seminars. We normally provide details of our recommended power team at the live seminars that we run. You will find that you will meet some professionals who tell you that they can help you, and do exactly what you want, but then when it comes to the crunch they don't know what they are doing. So if you are going to put your own team together, do expect that there may be an element of trial and error until you find the right team;

it may take you some time, but once you've got it right you will be able to concentrate on finding the great deals.

Who should be in your power team?

Initially, you will start with a core power team consisting of the essential people you need to make the deals happen. With time, you will probably develop an extended power team who will help you systematise the process and give you more free time to focus on what you want to do.

Your Core Power Team

This will include a property specialist tax accountant, a mortgage broker and solicitors. Let's consider each of these in turn.

Your property specialist tax accountant:

It is very important to get the correct tax advice to make sure that you keep as much as possible of the money that you make from property by minimising the amount of tax you pay. When it comes to property investing, most accountants will understand the basics but may not have the specialist property tax knowledge required. Everyone is different and so you need to get specialist advice tailored to your specific requirements and needs. Your property specialist tax accountant will be able to help advise you in the set up of your property business(s) and also should be consulted on all major transactions such as disposal of property or structuring of joint ventures, etc. The correct advice could save you a fortune, so it is well worth paying for some quality personal advice.

My criteria for selecting a property tax accountant are as follows. They need to be:

- A property tax specialist

- A property investor themselves

Your mortgage broker:

Probably one of the most important people in your power team, your mortgage broker is your access to finance. Your broker needs to understand explicitly what you are doing. Don't assume that all mortgage brokers are the same.

My criteria for selecting a mortgage broker are as follows. They need to be:

- Fully independent with access to the entire mortgage market

- Dealing with BTL mortgages and re-mortgages on a daily basis

- Able to respond quickly to your needs

- Investing in property themselves

Some mortgage brokers will charge you a fee and some will work for you free of charge. Amateur investors often make the mistake of trying to save money by going to the cheapest supplier. Experience shows this is not always the best option. I am a firm believer that you get what you pay for. However, if you are dealing with the broker on a regular basis, they should be prepared to negotiate their fee. The best way to find a good mortgage broker, as with most members of your power team, is through personal recommendation from other investors who use their services. There are some great mortgages brokers who attend the pin meetings each month.

Your solicitors:

You will need two different solicitors to complete your property purchase. One solicitor will represent you in the purchase and a second, separate solicitor will represent the seller in the sale. I have had a number of experiences where the deal has almost fallen through because the seller's solicitor was simply not very good. As I cannot afford to risk this, sometimes I offer to cover the cost of the seller's solicitor, as long as the seller uses the solicitor that I recommend. The solicitor that I recommend will, of course, have to act in the best interest of the seller. However, I know the solicitor that I recommend has a good working relationship with the solicitor representing me, and so I can ensure the transaction will happen in the required time, which benefits everyone.

My criteria for selecting solicitors are as follows. They need to be:

- Friendly and contactable with a good response rate

- Proactive, rather than reactive which is what most solicitors are

- Able to carry out all transactions over the phone and by email for speed

- Able to work with the other solicitors in an efficient manner

- Cost-effective for the service they provide

Your Extended Power Team

Over time, you will develop your extended power team which may include the following: estate agents, letting agents, builders, property finders and coaches, to name just a few. Let's consider some of these:

Estate agents:

As discussed in Chapter 3, estate agents can be a great source of potentially motivated sellers for you. I have a number of estate agents who call me first when they find the right kind of deal. In addition to sourcing property for you, the same estate agents can help you sell the properties which you want to buy and flip on. It is well worth investing the time to build up good relationships with the right kind of estate agents.

Letting agents:

Employing a good letting agent can save you a lot of time and hassle. Unfortunately, many letting agents aren't very good, but if you know how to find them, there are some good ones out there. Letting agents can also be a good source of motivated seller leads for you because if any of their landlords decide to sell a property, the letting agents are often the first people to find out about it. If you have a good relationship with your agent this could be another source of leads for you. You may not require letting agents to manage a property for you, but they can be very useful in helping to find the tenants. It is not a good use of your time to manage your own properties. Again, your local pin meeting could be a great place to meet a good local letting agent.

Property finders:

As well as finding your own motivated seller leads, you may well have a number of other property investors and property finders who are out looking at deals for you. This is particularly useful if you're working full-time and just can't afford the time to do it yourself. You will have to pay them a fee, but if it means you get to build up a property portfolio with very little effort, it can be well worth it.

Insurance specialist:

As a landlord it is very important that you have the correct landlord insurance in place. Not only do you need to have appropriate cover for the buildings and your contents in the property but also public liability insurance in case someone has an accident in your property and then decides that it was your fault and so tries to sue you. If you are selling property deals to other people, then you should also have professional indemnity insurance.

Call answering service:

Whenever you are contacted by a motivated seller, you need to speak to them in person. If a seller goes through to your answerphone, most of them will be reluctant to leave a message as they don't really know who you are. Rather than leaving a message, it is more likely that the seller will just move on to the next property problem solver, and you may have missed out on a potential deal. If you are constantly busy on your phone or unable to answer it during the day, you need to make provision for someone else to answer on your behalf. Whoever answers the phone for you must have a script so they know exactly what to say and can capture all the required information.

Virtual assistant:

You will soon come to realise that there are lots of things that you need to do as a property investor, but the good news is that you do not need to do everything yourself. There are lots of tasks you can get other people to do for you, especially things like admin where a well-trained virtual assistant can save you a huge amount of time. As time is your most valuable asset, you need to delegate as much as you can to other people, so that you can focus on the most important tasks where you can add the most value such as finding great property deals.

Builders:

If you are adding value to properties through renovation work, you will need professional builders to carry out the work for you. Remember, it is not worth your time doing this work yourself, so it's best to pay a professional to do it properly. The best way to build up a good relationship with your builder is to pay them promptly. Builders always seem to be chasing people for money, so if you pay them promptly in full, you will become one of their favoured clients and they may well then prioritise your jobs over those of others.

Handyman:

You may need someone to keep an eye on your properties and carry out small jobs of maintenance and repair. Having a local multi-skilled handyman who is available to attend to your properties at short notice can be really useful.

Property coach or mentor:

Once you get to a certain number of properties you may find it very difficult to talk to family and friends about what you're doing. They just won't understand it, and this is the point at which you need a property coach or mentor who can help stretch you, give you support and guidance and keep you motivated.

Now that we have considered the type of people you need in your power team, you may want to think about the gaps in your current team. Who else do you need in your team? How are you going to find them?

Management of your properties

I am not going to spend too much time talking about the management of your properties in this book, as I want to focus on the motivated seller purchase strategies instead. Besides, there are plenty of excellent books all about property management that do a far better job that I would do. You can find some of my personal property management book recommendations on our free resources webpage:

www.Property-Mastermind.co.uk/resources

However, it is very important that once you purchase your investment property, you quickly fill it with good tenants who will cover all the costs and make a monthly cash profit for you.

There is one point I would like to make about managing your property portfolio as follows.

When I first started to invest in property, I wanted to personally manage all of my properties as they were within five minutes' drive of where I lived in Birmingham. I found that managing a few properties did not take too much time and I actually enjoyed it. To be honest, I thought that I could do a better job than most agents and I did not want to give a letting agent 10% of my rental income. If you are already a landlord, then I am sure that you have felt like this as well.

This was all fine until I fell into what I call the landlord trap. Managing a few properties was not very time consuming, but I found that the more properties I owned, then the more time I had to spend looking after them, which meant that I had less time to focus on buying properties and my acquisition rate dramatically slowed. I was making good income from my property but it was far from passive, as I had become a full-time property manager. I realised that I had swapped my job at Cadbury, which I had really enjoyed, for a job as a property manager, which I was not passionate about. This was ironic, as the whole point of me investing in property was to give me a passive income so that I was free to do the things I wanted to do. This is when I decided to hand over all of the management of my properties to a good letting agent. It meant that I took a short-term dip in income but I was able to get all of my time back. I was then able to concentrate on buying property and thus quickly replaced the income shortfall and, in fact, far superseded my former corporate salary.

I understand the desire to manage your first few properties, but believe me the novelty soon wears off. I encourage all of my students to make sure that they account for the cost of someone else managing their property when they do the calculation to assess if they should purchase a property or not. You can still manage your property if you really want to, but that is not why most people get into property investing in my experience.

The challenge can be in finding a good letting agent who really knows what they are doing and will look after your property and your tenants for you. I find the best way to do this is through word of mouth recommendation. Ask other investors in your area who they use and what their experience is of that agent. A great place to meet other investors and letting agents is at property networking meetings. If you look in the back of this book in Chapter 8, there are details of how you can attend one of the property investor network meetings as my guest on your first visit, and save yourself the normal £20 entry fee.

The quicker you can get someone else managing your properties for you the sooner you can enjoy your new-found freedom that property investing can give you.

Widen your possibilities through joint ventures

To become a really successful investor you need to think bigger than just what you can do on your own. Working with other investors in joint ventures can give you access to a greater number and variety of investment opportunities. A joint venture can give you:

- Access to knowledge and experience

- Money to fund the project

- Time to find great deals

- Better networks of suppliers and contacts

A joint venture makes the most of leverage, so that there is no limit to what you can achieve with the right joint venture partners. When you get a reputation for being very good at what you do, you will find that people will bring deals to you. One of the benefits that I gain from teaching other investors how to invest successfully is that I get exposure to thousands of potential joint venture partners every year. Occasionally, investors bring great deals back to me that they feel they cannot do on their own and they want to use my expertise to make sure the deal happens. This works very well for all the parties involved.

Joint venture partners generally fall into two categories. You have the people who are 'cash rich and time poor' and the people who are 'time rich but cash poor'. Which category do you fall into? Maybe you are reading this book and thinking that you are both 'cash poor and time poor!' Don't worry, you can still do deals but you just need to think smart and work very creatively.

CASE STUDY:
Dick Dabner

I have been an entrepreneur all my life and I was delighted when my son Peter joined the family business when he left school. We worked hard for 10 years together in the glass industry, expanding into manufacturing and retail. In the late 1990s we had four properties between us, one investment property each and the homes in which we each lived.

One day in 2002, going through the glass business figures after a particularly tough period of trading, it occurred to us that we had done better from the capital growth gained in the four properties than we had in the past 12 months working 60 hours a week in our 'day jobs', and the properties had taken only a few hours of management all year.

We made the decision to close down the glass business and concentrate on property full time. At that point, we had bank overdrafts and personal guarantees from the business that needed to be repaid, so we were highly motivated to start on property because we were determined to repay what we owed as quickly as possible.

We sold two properties to repay some debt and put the third property up for sale, but then we did a property course and learned that we could refinance the remaining two properties, which would leave us with enough to put down the deposit on a small one-bed flat, which we bought with a Buy-to-Let mortgage.

We purchased this flat below market value and did a 'makeover' type of refurbishment, making sure that we 'added value', establishing the principle of making money by using this strategy. We knew that other flats in good order locally were selling for £120k to £130k.

Our business plan was basic: buy for £92k and finish the refurbishment for less than £8k , keeping the total to less than £100k. We then had the flat re-valued and took another mortgage to refinance. It was surveyed and the new valuation came back at £125k. We had made £25k of equity in a few weeks!

Peter had been looking for other properties with which we could use the same strategy and had been offered both the flat next door and the flat opposite, so we agreed to buy both at £93k each. We had no money of our own to expand and buy these properties, but we knew that there was another £50k waiting for us, as long as we could come up with the funds to buy these other two flats.

We started to speak to friends and family, telling them about what we were doing, and we soon found our first two joint venture business partners who were prepared to put up the money in return for an interest rate or a share of the profit, with the promise that if it all went to plan, there was more money available.

This gave us the confidence to buy the two flats, which we could sell after refurbishing them. They were then surveyed at £124k and £135k respectively and we were able to repay our investors including their profit.

We had made some money and, more importantly, we had also established the two principles that have worked for us ever since, no matter what the market conditions are: interest payment or profit share. As long as we find joint venture partners, identify good deals and add value to the property, we can make money for ourselves and for our investors whether the market is going up, down or sideways!

Our latest joint venture project was the purchase of a semi-detached property on a large plot with a workshop. The seller was in financial difficulty and the property was about to be repossessed. The property, which was on the market for £325k, had been sold twice, only for the sale to fall through both times. We spotted the massive development opportunity for the site and decided to see if we could help this seller. We agreed a purchase price of £250k and stepped in to stop the repossession.

We managed to get a lock-out agreement which meant we could get into the property before exchange to do a simple refurbishment and also start the planning application. We then exchanged contracts on the condition that the deposit was used to clear the arrears to make sure the property did not get repossessed. We had a delayed completion which gave us more time to get the planning approval.

We achieved planning permission to convert the semi-detached property into two two-bed flats (worth £330k), the workshop into a two-bed house (worth £240k), and to build a pair of semi-detached properties on the plot (worth £300k each). This means the total development value of the site is £1.17m. One of our JV partners put in about £400,000 for the building work. After all the costs, our profit from this one purchase will be about £300k which we will split with our JV partners.

Now we have an established portfolio with a good rental income stream, and we are able to use this to pay interest to JV partners so that we can continue to expand.

We always pay far more than the banks, so that we find more new investors and most of them become long-term joint venture partners. We know that, with their help, we can undertake far more projects in property than we could ever do on our own, and that way everybody wins.

Since discovering the power of working with other people, I have continued to expand my knowledge and experience in property by investing in my own education. Many of the strategies I now use for finding properties to buy and for structuring deals have come directly or indirectly from participating in the Property Mastermind Programme and simply following the course and taking action in line with my goals. This has enabled me to prosper despite the adverse financial climate and I believe that joint ventures will provide continuing success in the future.

Working successfully with other people

Whenever you work with other people in a team or as partners in a joint venture, ideally everyone should bring different skills and talents into the team. This means you can focus on what you are naturally good at, where you can add the most value and find other people who are excellent at the things that you are not so good at. This makes working with other people easier and more enjoyable.

To help the delegates on my Property Mastermind Programme we use a number of different profiling tests which help the delegates identify their natural talents and work out who specifically they should be working with to get the best results for all involved.

Since introducing these profiling tests we have seen the results achieved by our delegates significantly improve, because they are far more effective in selecting the right partners to work with so that they can complement each other's skills and talents.

You can find out how you can benefit from this profiling here: www.Property-Mastermind.co.uk/Profile

Elements of successful joint ventures

For a joint venture to work you have to select the right partners. First of all, each partner needs to bring something different to the partnership. It is really important to have an open and honest relationship. You should always start with clear, simple documents that outline how the partnership will work. You need to understand who is responsible for what in the partnership. As part of this agreement, you need to have a clear exit strategy, so you know exactly how and when the partnership will finish. You should also consider scenario analysis and contingency planning just in case things don't go to plan.

How to use your equity at no cost to you

I regularly meet investors who tell me they have no money to invest. Very often, after some questioning, we discover that actually they do have plenty of money to invest, if they use the equity in their own home. The problem here is that many amateur investors do not want to use the equity from existing property for two reasons. First of all, they think it may be a risk, and secondly, they recognise that there is a cost to do this and they may be concerned about funding that cost.

Releasing equity from your own property is a great way to raise funds to invest in property and there are ways you can do it at no cost to you. Before I explain this idea, I must remind you that I'm not a regulated financial adviser. This does not constitute financial advice – I am merely suggesting some possibilities to you.

Imagine you own a property that has at least £100k of equity that you could release. The cost of releasing this equity will depend on interest rates at the time, but let's assume that you could release equity at a cost of 3% per annum. This £100k would cost you £3k in interest per year, or £250 per month. Assume you meet another investor with whom you develop a working relationship. You may decide to go into a joint venture partnership on a project with them. If you lend the joint venture partner half of your £100k, but then charge them 6% (double the rate that you are paying), then the interest that they pay you on the £50k you lend them will cover your cost of borrowing on the full £100k.

This means that you will have the remaining £50k, which you can use to invest with the assurance that the cost of borrowing the money is covered by someone else.

The person who borrows the money also gets a great deal because it is far easier to borrow from a private individual than it is to borrow from a bank or lending institution. Of course, you need to pick your partner carefully, as you would not want to lend your money to just anybody. Make sure they know what they are doing. Also make sure you put your agreement in writing, so that everyone is clear about their obligations, and get some form of security such as a personal guarantee.

How to find a suitable joint venture partner

There are potential joint venture partners all around you! They could be family, friends or other investors. Some of those people may not know that they are your potential JV partners at the moment, because they do not fully understand what property investing can do for them.

One of the first things you should do is to educate them. This may not be easy if you are new to investing yourself as they may think, "What do you know about property?". A simple step would be to give them a copy of this book and tell them that you found it really interesting and think they will too. As long as they read it and you follow up, they may well be more inclined to have a discussion about how you could work together.

When you are looking for a potential joint venture partner, you need to consider what you have to offer, what you require and what is really important to you. Once you have worked this out, you need to look through your network of investors to identify a suitable partner – someone who has what you need and who needs what you have.

When you meet a potential partner, you need to find out what is really important to them. This is why it's important to network with other investors and build quality relationships. Once you have identified a suitable partner, you need to consider the type of deals in which you both want to be involved. I usually look at each joint venture proposal on its own individual merits. I decide if I want to get involved in a project and then communicate it to suitable partners who I already know will be interested in that type of venture. I consider all the potential partners and decide who I think would be best to get involved in that particular project, and then we set up a deal that is a win/win solution for both of us.

What should be in a joint venture agreement?

I'm often asked this question, but the reality is that you can make it anything you want, as long as it works for all the parties involved. I think it is important to have the agreement in writing, as there is a danger that there could be confusion in the future around a verbal agreement. The best advice I would give you is to keep it simple and straightforward. Basically, you need to include some information about the project outline and objectives, and clearly detail who is responsible for what. You need to detail the inputs from each partner, the timescales and deadlines involved. You also need to consider the financial arrangements and cash flow requirements of the project, as well as the expected returns, profit share and risk analysis. This might sound like a lot of detail but it could easily be covered on a few sheets of A4 paper.

In conclusion to this chapter, you don't have to do everything on your own. You must value your time and remember that people with a rich mindset will spend their money to save time. I recommend that you focus on the things that you enjoy and that you are good at, and delegate all the other tasks to someone else who can do them better than you. With this in mind, who can you get to help you?

Chapter 8:

The best investment you can make!

Invest in yourself

Investing time and effort in your own education and personal development is the best investment you will ever make.

The knowledge and skills you gain through education will stay with you for the rest of your life. For the majority of the population, the only education they get is the formal education they receive at school, college or even university.

Unfortunately, this traditional form of education does absolutely nothing to teach you the fundamentals of life about money, finance and investing. Most people learn the hard way by making mistakes, which is a very expensive way to learn. A far easier, quicker and cheaper way to learn is from someone else who has already become successful, from whom you can learn from their successes, and also from their mistakes.

Since 1998, I have invested in my own personal development and ongoing education. I'm constantly looking to improve myself, my skills and expertise. I believe you never stop learning, if only you are open to it. Without appearing to sound arrogant, I know that I'm very knowledgeable in the area of residential property investing. I have over two decades of experience. I've made a lot of money, but also made a lot of mistakes. However, I don't claim to know it all. I am still learning and, because I'm involved in property investing every day, I learn something new every day. I'm always looking to learn from other successful investors and improve on what I do. I've noticed that the most successful people are also the most open-minded. I have coached and trained many thousands of investors since 2003 and I have observed that some of the hardest people to teach are often those who have some experience. Sometimes, due to their experience they believe they know it all. A little knowledge can be a dangerous thing. It is very frustrating when someone says or thinks "I know", because they are closing down their mind to new possibilities and opportunities.

The point is, why would you want to learn the hard way, wasting your time, money and effort, when you can easily learn from someone else who has already been successful and can show you how to avoid the mistakes that most investors will make? I think one of the problems is that most people are not prepared to put the time, effort or money into educating themselves. I must admit, I myself was very sceptical before I got into personal development.

I remember my first exposure to personal development when I was about 24 and I wasn't very impressed. In hindsight, perhaps I wasn't really ready for it at that age. I was in a friend's car on a journey from Birmingham to London. As it was his car and he was driving, he insisted that we listen to his new Anthony Robbins personal development cassette tapes. I would rather have listened to the radio, but I didn't really mind and I suppose I was a little bit curious. I only half listened as I probably dozed off, but I just did not get it at the time. I think my friend got more of a reaction from me when he told me how much he had paid for this personal development audio pack... £50! I could not believe it!

£50 seemed like a lot of money to me at the time. I remember thinking to myself, "Why would anyone spend £50 on a set of audio cassettes?" It's amazing how people change. Six years later, at a live Anthony Robbins event, I signed up for his Mastery University, which was well over $10,000 at the time. That investment in myself changed my life.

Nowadays, I think nothing of spending thousands of pounds to go to a seminar, sometimes even travelling to the other side of the world, because I know if I get just one good idea, it will be time and money well invested. I am selective about which seminars or courses I attend, but each year I commit to spending a certain amount of income and time developing myself further. I really enjoy learning, growing and stretching my thinking to help me perform at a higher level. I understand the value of paying for information and expertise.

I am confident that, if for any reason I were to lose everything, I would be able to get back to where I am now much quicker, faster and easier than I did the first time, because I know exactly what to do this time and, maybe more importantly, what not to do. How about you? Are you investing enough in yourself? Do you have the skills and knowledge you need to be a successful property investor?

What skills do you need to be a successful investor?

Mental attitude: I firmly believe that you can have all the skills, knowledge and strategies in the world, but these are useless if you don't have the right investor's mindset. To be a successful investor you need to have the right attitude and the self-belief that you can achieve anything you put your mind to. Most investors think that investing is all about the strategies and techniques you use. I personally believe that the strategies are 20% and your attitude and mindset are 80% of what it takes to be a really successful investor.

Positive outlook: Are you generally a positive or a negative person? I know we all go through phases, and sometimes we have bad days, but I promise you it is easier to achieve what you want if you're positive and looking for the possibilities rather than looking for negatives and what can't be done. You get what you think about and focus on. As a property problem solver, you need to be very creative, with a solution-focused outlook. There is always a way. Your role is often to solve problems by finding solutions that other people cannot see.

Listening skills: The best way to help a motivated seller is to ask them what they want and listen to what they tell you. As simple as this sounds, all too often I hear of investors who talk at motivated sellers rather than talking with them. Building rapport and a trusting relationship is absolutely critical if you want to help these people and secure a good win/win deal. You need to become good at asking questions and listening to the answers to make sure you really understand the situation and find the best possible solution for you and the motivated seller.

Research skills: Whenever you find a potential motivated seller lead, you need to act very quickly. Before you move on any deal, you need to quickly assess if it will work for you. Research is really important. You need to be able to determine the value of a property, the rental potential and realistic rental income that it might achieve. Luckily, it is extremely easy and quick to do this with the use of the internet and a telephone. When you know how, it can take just twenty minutes to obtain a realistic valuation that a chartered surveyor would also arrive at using like comparisons of similar properties.

Numerical skills: Property investing is all about the numbers and return on your investment. You need to be able to work out if a deal stacks up or not. We cover this in Chapter 5. Luckily, you don't have to do this in your head or on the spot, but you do need to understand the numbers upon which you will base your investing decisions.

Negotiation skills: As I maintain throughout this book, you need to come up with a solution that is a win/win for both you and the seller. You need to be ethical and make sure that you do not take advantage of the seller's situation. Having said that, the deal has to work for you otherwise there is no point doing it. Remember, this is a business. In most motivated seller purchases there is some scope for negotiation. The level of your negotiation skills can dramatically impact the profitability of your business.

Self discipline: To be successful we sometimes need to push ourselves and do things outside our comfort zone. It can be very easy to use excuses as to why we have not done something, but really it just comes down to being disciplined and focused on what you want. We may need to make some short-term sacrifices in order to achieve and enjoy long-term benefits.

Having the discipline to do something each day to move you towards your goals will have a massive positive impact on your results. Have a look in the resources section of the website which has some great book recommendations for you on this.

Persistence: This is probably one of the most important skills you can develop. Investing in property is not easy. There are lots of challenges and obstacles you will need to overcome. Unfortunately, most people give up far too easily, often just before they achieve the results they are looking for. You need to keep going and remember that if other people have been successful and found a way there is no reason why you can't do the same.

Looking at your current skills set compared to the skills required to be a successful property problem solver, where do you feel that you may need to improve your skills? What can you do to improve your skills?

Remember, you don't have to be good at everything. You can get other people to help you in areas in which you are not so strong. Working with other people is much smarter than doing it on your own, which can be very lonely.

The smart way to educate yourself

Now that we have recognised the need to constantly improve yourself and develop your skills, knowledge and experience, there are several ways in which you can achieve this. You need to select the methods that best fit with your time and personal requirements. Here are a few ideas for you:

Networking: There are now many very good specialist networking groups for property investors. Attending these events on a regular basis is one of the best ways to develop your knowledge by mixing with and learning from other successful investors. This is the main reason I founded the

Property Investors Network (pin) back in 2003. I recognised the incredible value that I had personally gained by learning from and networking with other successful investors. Networking is a low-cost way of gaining knowledge in terms of financial input, but it does require some time, effort and dedication from you.

The more investors you know and the bigger your network, the more opportunities you will become aware of. There are property investor groups all over the UK. I suggest you use the internet to find a group near to where you live or work and start visiting on a regular basis. This is also a great way to keep yourself motivated and on track. Property investing can be lonely sometimes, especially if your friends and family don't really understand what you do. You need to be around like-minded people who can give you support, encouragement and advice. We hold property investor network meetings in major cities around the UK every month. To find out about your local pin meeting you can visit: www.PinMeeting.co.uk.

Educational seminars and courses: There are a number of individuals and companies in the UK who provide property investing education. Some of them are better than others and it is up to you to decide which is best for you. Seminars are a great way for you to learn a lot of information very quickly. Although you often have to pay to attend these seminars, the knowledge that you gain will make the investment of time and money very worthwhile.

To be honest, given enough time and research, you could probably discover for yourself most of the information that you will learn at a seminar. However, the main reason you attend a seminar is to obtain a lot of information, compressed into a very short amount of time, instead of having to spend months reading books, looking on the internet and speaking to other investors. You need to start valuing your time and recognise when you are spending time and when you are investing time. This comes back to mental attitude. Amateur investors with a poor mindset will spend their time to save money, whereas investors with a rich mindset will always spend their money to save time. Rich people realise that time is their most valuable asset.

One tip that I would give you is that you need to make sure the presenter who is sharing their knowledge is actively investing themselves. Do they have practical experience or are they just teaching you theory that they have learned from a book? Make sure they are 'walking their talk'. Also, it is important to find someone who has become very good at transferring their knowledge and experience to other people. You want to train with someone who has got plenty of successful students whose footsteps you can follow in. Also be wary of the companies who run seminars to get you all excited about property investment and at the end of the seminar want you to sign up at the back of the room to buy properties there and then. Now, these may be perfectly good investment opportunities, but how do you know that? You should never buy any property investment just because you see other people buying it. You always need to do your own research before you decide to buy anything. That does not mean you should take a long time to decide, it just means you need to do your research thoroughly and quickly to decide if the opportunity is right for you. I have made a video all about how to find the best property training for you which you can watch on the free pin App. Details of how to download this App come later in this chapter.

Home study: If you can't seem to make the time to attend live seminars, or the dates and locations just don't work for you, then home study could be a good solution. There are plenty of online video and audio courses that you can invest in, which means you can fit in learning around your lifestyle. If you spend a lot of time travelling to and from work rather than listening to the radio, you could use this time productively by listening to an educational audio.

Coaches or mentors: Reading books or attending seminars to learn how to invest in property is pointless unless you put your knowledge into practice. One of the best ways of doing this is to have a coach who will support you, help you to take action and hold you to account. Your coach should be someone who is more experienced than you and can add value to your investing, help you to grow and expand your knowledge. Your coach must have a proven track record and ideally should be recommended to you by another successful investor. Some of the most successful graduates from my Property Mastermind Programme have gone on to become property coaches in their own right. We now have trained and accredited coaches who provide coaching support, accountability and guidance for delegates on my Property Mastermind Programme and attendees at pin meetings.

Mastermind groups: As you may recall, one of my hobbies from an early age was performing magic tricks. I used to save all my pocket money and then make a trip to London about twice a year with my Dad to visit the world-famous Davenports Magic shop. In 1982, Davenports relocated from Great Russell Square to the Charing Cross Underground shopping concourse where, as well as the shop, they also had a magic studio in which they would hold magic lectures and shows. They also started a Saturday morning club for young magicians called the Demon Magic Club. I went to the very first Demon Magic Club meeting and got hooked. It became a regular Saturday event for the next five years or so. Each week we would learn a new trick from a professional magician, practise it and work on the presentation. Not only would we learn from the professional but also from each other. The result was that we all experienced an exponential rise in our presentation, confidence and ability. There was an incredibly supportive environment, and when I look back at it now I realise this was actually the first mastermind group that I was a member of.

Later in life, when I started my personal development journey through Anthony Robbins, I was reminded of the importance of environment to help you achieve your goals. To speed up your success you need to mix with positive, like-minded people and ideally find other people who have achieved what you want and then model them. I have taken these lessons and applied them since 2003 to the property training that we now provide in a number of different formats to suit anybody who wants to be a more successful property investor.

I myself am a member of a number of mastermind groups and I am very proud of all the investors we have helped to change their lives as part of the 12-month Property Mastermind Programme, which I first launched in April 2007.

Further learning with me

The purpose of this book is raise your awareness of what is possible, and inspire you to change your life for the better, whilst helping other people solve their property problems.

I sincerely hope that you have enjoyed reading *Property Magic*, found it inspirational and have learned a great deal from it. When I sat down to write it, my objective was to share with you some of the incredible learning that I've gained through teaching the motivated seller purchase strategies to my Property Mastermind Programme delegates.

I have deliberately kept the strategy explanations as simple as possible, and I believe that you have enough information to decide if the motivated seller strategy is appropriate for you. Personally, I believe that this strategy is perfect for anyone who is interested in building a significant portfolio in a relatively short amount of time. Knowledge alone is useless; you need to put your knowledge and skills into action.

Although the case studies in this book are all based in the UK, the principles of finding motivated sellers, and helping them to solve their property problems for mutual benefit, works anywhere in the world. I have clients in Europe, Asia, the Middle East and Australia who have all successfully used these strategies in their own countries. Of course, in other countries mortgages, taxes, and legal systems may well be different, but the fact remains that there are motivated sellers everywhere, you just have to find them and look to solve their problems.

There is only so much information I can share in a book. I would like to share with you details of how I believe I can help you further on your property investing journey. I want to hold your hand and help you to make the journey smoother, quicker and more enjoyable than if you try to do it on your own. So for your information, here is the further training and support we can help provide for you.

Further resources for you

We have set up a special webpage for you with information about further resources to use, including:

- Links to useful websites and tools

- Other recommended books

- Special offers and discounts from recommended service providers

- Exclusive offers for *Property Magic* readers

You can access all of these further resources at this webpage: www.Property-Mastermind.co.uk/resources

The pin App

We have created a free App for your mobile phone which contains hours of video training on strategies such as Rent to Rent, Purchase Lease Options, Houses of Multiple Occupation, as well as how to find and deal with motivated sellers.

There is also a listing of all 50+ property investor network monthly meetings, including locations, dates and details of the property experts who are speaking at your local pin meeting that month.

The App is called "Successful Property Investing" which you can download direct from the app store. Or, for your convenience, here are the links to type into your smartphone/ device depending on the type you have.

With your iPhone just click on this link: http://bit.ly/pinAPP1

With your Android phone use this link: https://bit.ly/pinAPP2

Property Investors Network (pin)

– monthly networking evenings

The purpose of pin is to provide a support environment in which you can continue to learn more about successful property investing. Every month we host evening networking events in most major cities around the UK. There are two fundamental aspects to these monthly meetings:

1) Networking and 2) Education. These events give you a great opportunity to meet, learn from, and network with other successful investors. Each month we cover a different investing topic in the educational seminars. I am delighted to say that we consistently attract some of the top UK property investing experts to speak at our events.

Most people arrive from 6.00p.m. for informal networking. The educational seminar runs from 7.00p.m. until about 9.00p.m., after which informal networking continues. I recommend you come along to your local pin meeting to check it out for yourself. You need to reserve your place in advance online.

All of the monthly events, dates and locations are listed here: www.PinMeeting.co.uk

As my gift to you, if you have never been to a pin meeting, I would like to invite you to attend your first local pin meeting as my guest, completely free of change. Normally entry is just £20 per person, but if you follow the easy steps outlined below, there will be no charge for your first visit.

- Go to www.PinMeeting.co.uk

- Choose which pin meeting you would like to attend, and click on that link to check the date, location and details of the next meeting

- Scroll down the page to the 'Select a Payment Option' and click on 'Book with a Voucher Code'

- Then enter your name, email address and mobile number, along with this voucher code "Magic6"

- Next click on the 'Click here to book your place now' button

- Your name will be added to the guest list and an email confirmation will be sent to you

It really is a very friendly environment and the host will make you feel welcome and help you to get the most out of the experience. Why not check out the website now to find your local meeting and book yourself in as my guest?

Pin Academy – online resource for property investors

Pin Academy is a private membership website which brings together the very best elements of the extensive pin network for you to make the most of your online and offline networking.

As a member of Pin Academy there are four key benefits for you:

Member only private Facebook group

Access the collective knowledge and contacts from over 1,000 other members. Connect, share and learn in this safe online community! Get all your property questions answered.

Online 24/7 video training

Access online video training whenever you want, including our "Your Property Journey" 10-week online training programme and highlights from some of our specialist online training including, BMV purchasing, Purchase Lease Options and House of Multiple Occupation (HMO's).

Monthly webinars and replays

Each month we run a number of different webinars, some of which are exclusive to Pin Academy members. If you can't join us for the live webinars, you can benefit from watching the webinar replays whenever you want and get access to our extensive back catalogue.

Complimentary access to pin meetings

There are now 50+ pin meetings each month (apart from August and December). You can gain complimentary access to as many of these meetings as you want each month as a Pin Academy member.

You can join Pin Academy either monthly or annually. To find out more about how you can benefit as a member of Pin Academy and to take advantage of the exclusive membership offer for *Property Magic* readers, visit this website now:

www.PinAcademy.co.uk/Magic

The Ultimate Property Investors Bootcamp – audio programme

This best-selling, study-at-home audio programme provides a solid foundation for anyone who is serious about investing in property. Guest speakers on this programme include some of the top property investing experts in the UK and all of my personal power team. With over 10 hours of audio material, this is an incredibly detailed programme which covers the following topics:

- Why you should be investing in property!

- Planning your strategy and conducting research

- Fundamentals of property investing

- Understanding finance and taxation

- How to profit from Property Options

- Benefits of networking and Joint Ventures

- Buying property from estate agents and auctions

- Buying property from motivated sellers

- Letting your property

- Maximising the rent on your property

- Advanced Investing Strategies

- How to take your investing to the next level

For full details of exactly what you'll learn on this audio programme, visit this website:

www.Property-Mastermind.co.uk/Bootcamp

All of our products come with a 100% money back guarantee. If you don't think this is the best property investing course you've enrolled on, simply return the entire package to us within 30 days and receive your money back in full.

Personality profiling test

In Chapter 7 I mentioned the profiling tests, which we put all of our Property Mastermind delegates through.

Since introducing these profiling tests we have seen the results achieved by our delegates significantly improve, because they are far more effective in selecting the best investing strategy and the right partners to work with so that they can complement each other's skills and talents.

You can find out how you can benefit from this profiling here: www.Property-Mastermind.co.uk/Profile

Property Magic Live

Property Magic Live is the big annual event hosted by me, at which successful investors from all over the UK come together each year to connect with each other and be inspired and learn the very latest strategies and what is working in the property market right now.

To find out about the next Property Magic Live event and to secure your tickets, visit the website today:

www.PropertyMagicLive.co.uk

Individual coaching and mentoring

Property Investors Network now offers a one-to-one private coaching service to help support you and hold you to account. The coaches are some of the most successful graduates from the Property Mastermind Programme whom I have personally selected and trained to be property investment coaches.

For full details of this service and to find a coach who can help you achieve your property goals, have a look at this webpage today. You will be able to book a complementary coaching session with one of our Mastermind Coaches:

www.Property-Mastermind.co.uk/Coaching

Mastermind Foundation

– one-day quick start seminar

I have created a special one-day seminar designed to teach you what you need to know to start buying property well below market value, right now. This seminar expands on some of the ideas shared in this book and explains exactly how to put the theory into practice.

By attending this Property Mastermind Foundation quick start seminar, you will learn the following:

- 28 reasons why vendors may be motivated to sell their property up to 40% below market value

- 20 strategies to find motivated sellers, including the quickest way to access them within 24 hrs without spending a penny

- How to deal with motivated sellers so that they want to sell to you instead of any other investors

- The five magic words to prove to sellers that you want to help them find an ethical win/win solution to their problem

- The negotiation strategy that could get an extra 20% discounted off the BMV price

- How to quickly evaluate a deal to decide if you should buy it or not

- How to use Momentum Investing to recycle your deposit which means that you can quickly build up your property portfolio

- How you can use other people's money as deposits if you run out your own source of finance

- Introduction to how to use Purchase Lease Options to control and profit from property that you don't own

- How to plan your exit strategy to minimise the tax liability and maximise your profit

Full details of this one-day quick start seminar, along with dates and locations, can be found on this website:

www.PropertyMastermindFoundation.co.uk

The Mastermind Accelerator 3-day workshop

This is an advanced, three-day, residential workshop in which we work through my Accelerator Investing Strategy Flow Chart and all the associated investing strategies.

This workshop is designed for the more advanced investor and is highly recommended for anyone who is considering joining the full Property Mastermind Programme.

Having spent three days with me (learning more than most investors learn in three years), you will subsequently know that the Property Mastermind Programme is perfect for you.

As usual there is a 100% money back guarantee to ensure that you have nothing to risk and everything to gain.

Full details of this advanced three-day workshop, along with dates and locations, can be found here: www.MastermindAccelerator. co.uk

The Property Mastermind Programme

I have mentioned my Property Mastermind Programme throughout this book, and now would be an appropriate time to tell you how the programme may be of benefit to you.

I have been teaching people how to successfully invest in property since 2003. One day in 2006 I was thinking about my business and made a radical decision: I decided that I wasn't going to run any more property investing seminars. This was a big decision because I really enjoyed speaking and teaching other people how to become financially independent, but I found myself becoming increasingly frustrated. Despite getting fantastic feedback from everyone who experienced my training, I was aware that there was a percentage of people who just didn't take action! I found this very frustrating and thought that maybe somehow it was my responsibility and so I stopped teaching to concentrate on my own investing.

During that period I made a lot of money in property, but to be honest, after six months I was bored. I then had a sudden realisation that it was the teaching and helping other people that I was passionate about, far more than investing. To me investing is just a vehicle to give me the financial independence to spend my time doing what I really love, which is speaking and teaching.

I made a decision that from then onwards I only wanted to work with serious investors who were going to take action on the valuable information I had to share with them.

After months of planning and research I came up with a blueprint for the Property Mastermind Programme. The initial idea came from the Mastermind principle, which Napoleon Hill talks about in his classic book *Think and Grow Rich*. With the help of my team and some of the UK's top property investing experts, we put together an outstanding, year-long, property investing mentorship, unique in the market, where it would be almost impossible not to succeed given all the support provided and accountability.

Our aim was to help anybody build a £1m property portfolio and achieve a £50k rental profit in just 12 months. With property values as they are today, a £1m property portfolio on its own is not that difficult, but the real challenge is the £50k profit after all expenses. Is this really possible? Absolutely! Since the very first Property Mastermind Programme back in April 2007, and on all the subsequent programmes to date, we have had delegates who have smashed this target of £1m in property and a £50k profit, sometimes in a lot less than 12 months, often from a standing start and with no money at all.

Has everyone been this successful? No, not everyone! Some people take a few years to achieve these sorts of results. As part of the Property Mastermind Programme, there is an accountability system to help support everyone and hold them to account.

Each year we run two, 12-month Property Mastermind Programmes, which start in April and October, with a maximum of 60 investors on each programme. We have an impressive track record of results achieved by both novice and experienced investors. Have a look at some of the success stories for yourself at:

www.Property-Mastermind.com/CaseStudies

The Property Mastermind Programme consists of eight key elements specifically designed to help you gain maximum benefit.

1. The Brain Transplant Pack

The Property Mastermind Programme has been designed for both new investors and experienced investors alike. Understandably, all of the delegates will be at different levels of knowledge, experience and confidence before they start the programme, so the first thing we do is help everyone get up to speed and be able to start from the same point. To achieve this, all participants receive the Brain Transplant Pack before the first workshop. This big pack of detailed information contains some of the very best property investing seminars I have run over the last few years, in written, audio and online video format, as well as some classic personal development programmes. If you were to purchase these products individually it would cost you almost £10k, but you get them included as a delegate on the Property Mastermind Programme. This gives you a solid base of property investing knowledge on which we build in the monthly advanced workshops.

2. Monthly Advanced One-Day Workshops

These are a fundamental part of the Property Mastermind Programme. At these advanced one-day events, you will experience an exponential growth in your knowledge, understanding and confidence thanks to the Mastermind principle and the input of everybody in the group. Networking and working together as a team will enable you to achieve far more than working on your own. We encourage delegates to share their successes and their learning to benefit the rest of the group.

Over the 12-month period there are 10 advanced workshops, one every month, with the exception of August and December. The content of each workshop is different and builds on the previous one. The content is constantly adapted and updated to account for changes in the property market.

It is really important that you commit to attend as many of these as possible. However, if you do happen to miss one or two, you can catch up by listening to the MP3s of the workshop that are made available to all of the delegates a week after each event.

By the end of each workshop, you will have a clear focus on exactly what you need to do before the next workshop, and a priority order in which your tasks need to be completed. There is an accountability system to make sure you take action and receive the maximum benefit from the learning experience.

Currently, delegates on the Property Mastermind Programme are from all over the UK and overseas, so for ease of access, all of the workshops are currently held at a hotel at the Birmingham NEC, just next door to Birmingham International Airport, Birmingham International train station and the M42.

3. The 24/7 support forum

This is an incredibly valuable private online forum which helps the Mastermind members to keep in touch on a daily basis. It is a great source of information for any questions you may have or assistance you need from other members of the group, as well as graduates from previous Mastermind Programmes who still have access to the forum. You can connect with past and present Mastermind delegates from all over the UK.

If you would like to have a sneak preview behind the scenes in our private forum, you can have a look at the short online video at this website:

www.Property-Mastermind.com/ForumDemo

4. Monthly support webinars

This element of the programme is designed to give you continued learning and direct access to me through monthly group coaching webinars. Each month I host at least one webinar, when you can ask me any questions you want. In these online sessions, we summarise the information from the previous workshop and I coach you through any challenges you may have. These calls will help you to keep motivated between the advanced workshops.

5. Your Mastermind Power Team

To be a successful investor you need to have the right team around you. As a delegate of the Property Mastermind Programme, you will have that team from day one, which means you don't have to waste your time or money finding your own team. On the advanced workshops, you will be introduced to the solicitors, mortgage brokers, property tax specialists, in fact all of my property power team whom I personally use to facilitate my property investing. Of course, you do not have to use my team, you can use anyone you want, however we have set up a team ready for you that works.

We also show you how to systematise your lead generation and handling system, so that even if you have a full-time job, you can make the Property Mastermind Programme work for you.

6. Lead Exchange and Joint Venture System

Using the online forum you will be able to offer your unwanted leads to other Mastermind members and purchase leads direct from them. By working as a group, you can have all of the Mastermind delegates out there looking for deals for you.

We always have a variety of different investors on the Mastermind Programme. Some of the investors are cash rich, but time poor. Some of them are cash poor, but time rich. By working together in joint ventures you can achieve far more than you could on your own with a lot less effort.

The best way to take advantage of these possibilities is to get to know the other members of the Mastermind Programme and, over time, build relationships with the individuals you want to work with. The online forum is the perfect place to find joint venture opportunities.

7. One-to-One Personal Success Coaching

To give you even more individual support and accountability, I have trained some of the most successful graduates from previous Mastermind Programmes to be able to give you monthly, private, one-to-one coaching calls. All of the coaches have successfully completed the Mastermind Programme and smashed the £1m of property and £50k profit targets. Think how much you will be able to achieve with the support of your own property investing coach holding you to account.

8. Two Days Mentoring Support

The final element of the Mastermind Programme is two days of personal property mentoring. This is where one of our successful coaches will visit you in your home town for two whole days to literally walk you through everything you need to do, step-by-step, to help you achieve your property goals.

Your recommended next steps

I hope that this has given you a brief overview of how the Property Mastermind Programme can help you achieve your property investing goals far more quickly and easily than if you try to do it on your own.

To find out more about the Property Mastermind Programme and to secure your place on the 'pre-announcement list' for the next available programme, simply visit this website now and register your interest for free:

www.Property-Mastermind.com/Magic

If you are new to investing, I recommend that you attend one of our Property Mastermind Foundation quick start seminars. This will give you the opportunity to dip your toe in the water and see if property investing is right for you.

If you are more experienced and want to learn the advanced strategies, then you should book yourself onto the next three-day Mastermind Accelerator workshop after which you will be absolutely clear if the full 12-month Property Mastermind Programme is perfect for you.

Mastermind Local

First launched in 2017, we also have the 12-month Property Mastermind Local, which is designed for people who wish to gain the benefits of being on the Mastermind Programme, but cannot physically make it to the advanced Mastermind workshops each month in Birmingham, due to time and/or geographical constraints. Instead of travelling to Birmingham each month, these smaller focused groups happen in various locations around the country. Full details here:

www.MastermindLocal.co.uk/Magic

Whatever you decide to do in property, remember you are not alone. You don't have to make all the mistakes yourself. You can learn from other people who have already been there, done it and made the mistakes so that you don't have to.

There is now so much information, resources and support available to you that there is no reason why you should not become a successful investor, if that is what you decide to do. I do hope that we will be able to help you further on your property investing journey.

So what do you do now?

With so many resources available to you, it can sometimes be confusing where to start, so I have put together a simple 4-step action list for you:

1. Register for and attend your next local pin meeting as soon as possible to keep your momentum going. Remember, if you have not been before, use voucher code "Magic6" to attend your first meeting, at no cost, as my guest. You can find your local meeting here: www.pinMeeting.co.uk

2. Complete the various profile tests which will give you direction and clarity on which might be the best strategies for you and how to find the right potential joint venture partners. Have a look here: www.Property-Mastermind.co.uk/Profile

3. If you are completely new to property investing, then the best thing would be to attend the next Property Mastermind Foundation one-day seminar to make sure you understand all the basics. You can book your place here now: www.PropertyMastermindFoundation.co.uk

4. If you want to speak to one of my team to discuss anything else including private coaching, Mastermind Accelerator, Mastermind Local or the full Mastermind Programme, then you can book a 20-minute strategy consultation in which they will help you identify the most effective route for you. Book your complimentary session here: www.property-mastermind.co.uk/Help

Chapter 9:

A few final words

It's a numbers game

Given that out of every 100 sellers only three or four of them may be motivated enough to give you the kind of deal you are looking for, you need to recognise that this is a numbers game. You will speak to lots of sellers and follow up lots of leads which may come to nothing. Not every lead you get will turn into a deal; however, every lead you do get is a great opportunity to practise your skills and develop them, so that when you get that 'deal of the decade' you are ready to take advantage of it. It would be a real shame to blow your first fantastic deal just because you don't have the experience to handle it. Experience comes with practice, patience and the application of your knowledge. Sometimes knowing where and how to start can be one of the biggest challenges.

Sowing the seeds

Once you have a really good understanding of how you can help motivated sellers, your first job is to set up your lead-generating system. This may be one of the hardest things you have to do as it does require some time and effort to get your systems up and running. Once they are in place they may only need a small amount of maintenance to keep the leads coming through to you.

Many of the lead-generation systems may take some time to start producing results. Some are quicker than others. For example, with a website and use of Google Adwords you could start generating leads instantly, whereas a leaflet campaign may take several weeks to organise and the response may come over a period of several months.

You need to be patient and have faith that as long as you've done the legwork, the leads will come to you. The more seeds you sow, the better results you will receive.

The only reason people fail is because they give up!

Investors, particularly when they are new to investing, get impatient. It is important for you to remember that property investing is a long-term investment. One of the great things about property is that you do the work once and you get paid forever! The one slight problem with this is that sometimes you don't get paid straightaway. You usually have to wait to enjoy the fruits of your labour.

In today's society everybody wants instant gratification; they want it all and they want it now. This means if people don't get the results they want in the time they expect, they often think that what they are doing just doesn't work and then they quit. Ironically this is often just before they would have achieved the results they desired; if only they had continued to persevere, rather than giving up.

This idea of giving up seems to be a behaviour we learn as adults. I think most people have a fear of failure (and some have a fear of success). We don't have that fear when we are kids. Did you learn to walk as a child? I am sure that to learn to walk you had to keep trying hundreds, if not thousands of times to get it right. When it didn't work, did you give up? After months of trying to walk without success, did your parents say to you, "Ah well, never mind, you might as well give up, you're never going to be able to walk"? No, of course not. They encouraged you. You kept at it. You persevered, learning from your mistakes, and eventually you learned to walk, something which you do now without even thinking about it.

At first, property investing may seem like a very daunting task. However, once you know the secret, just like magic, it's actually quite simple. With the correct strategy, some belief, positive action – oh, and somebody else's money – you can do it!

I look forward to hearing about your future success.

Best wishes, Simon Zutshi.

About the author

Simon Zutshi is a financially independent, professional property investor with over two decades of personal experience investing in residential property in the UK and overseas.

Simon started investing in 1995 when, as a first-time buyer and a recent graduate in debt, he found a strategy to purchase his first property (his own home) using none of his own money. By renting out the spare rooms, he was able to cover the mortgage payments and effectively live for free! Caught by the property bug, Simon started to buy more property and, by the age of 32, he was financially independent due to the passive income generated from his property portfolio.

Since an early age, Simon has been interested in the art of magic. He started to perform professionally at the age of 13 and became a member of the world-famous Magic Circle in his early 20's. Simon has often said that investing in property draws many parallels with magic, in that once you know the secret, what seemed impossible before is simple to achieve. As with any magic trick, knowing the secret is not always enough, and in order to become truly successful, you must practice and apply your knowledge with skill.

In 2003, Simon founded the Property Investors' Network, which is now a nationwide organisation, to provide a supportive environment for investors to learn more about investing, with the aim of maximising their return and minimising the risks.

Simon now spends most of his time helping and educating other investors by sharing his 'hands-on experience' gained over many years as a successful investor. He is one of the few property speakers in the UK who is a member of the Professional Speakers Association. As such, Simon is regularly invited to share his residential property investing strategies at the major property exhibitions and entrepreneurial business conferences in the UK and around the world.

In April 2007, Simon launched his Property Mastermind Programme, a 12-month mentoring programme designed to help you acquire an extra £1m of property, bringing you an annual profit in excess of £50k. Due to the accelerated learning techniques and supportive environment, many of the delegates on each programme achieve this goal in as little as 12 months. With an impressive track record of results achieved by its delegates, the Property Mastermind Programme has become so popular that Simon runs two of these programmes each year, starting in April and October.

To get an inside peek behind the scenes you can register your interest on the Property Mastermind website at:

www.Property-Mastermind.co.uk/Magic

You can also benefit from daily property investing hints and tips by following Simon on his social media:

Facebook: http://www.facebook.com/OfficialSimonZutshi

Lindkedin: https://www.linkedin.com/in/simonzutshi

Twitter:https://twitter.com/simonzutshi

YouTube: https://www.youtube.com/user/SimonZutshi